Hello Micha

All the Best !!

Jim
[signature]
6-15-23

"*The Decency Code* is an important book with a vital and timely message to leaders at all levels. Reading this book is an investment in building productive and engaged workplaces."

—MARSHALL GOLDSMITH,
#1 Leadership Thinker, Executive Coach,
and *New York Times* bestselling author

"Steve Harrison and Jim Lukaszewski have written a compelling business guide for leaders at every level who aspire to create cultures anchored around the values of civility . . . cultures that can convert discouraging workplaces into enabling, sustaining environments that ultimately outperform the competition."

—KEITH FERRAZZI, bestselling author of
Never Eat Alone and *Who's Got Your Back*

"*The Decency Code* reflects the authors' deep commitment to the role of integrity in contemporary leadership. They and their advocates will continue to be a global force in achieving the type of cultural transformation that defines excellence in business."

—MICHAEL C. BUSH,
CEO, Great Place to Work

"Why read this book about decency? While there are many big social issues in the world, every day we deal with others and have a chance to practice decency. Will this change the corporate world? It could help. But it can change you and help the people you deal with. And maybe, if we take this seriously, it can make a deep difference."

—JOE MURPHY, CCEP, Senior Advisor,
Compliance Strategists

"For more than 20 years, Jim Lukaszewski has been my single most trusted advisor and mentor for all matters of ethical corporate conduct and relentlessly positive communication. Jim and Steve share their secrets of wisdom in this outstanding manual of how to build the most decent of companies in today's challenging environment."

—SANDY DEAN, Chairman,
Mendocino and Humboldt Redwood Company, LLC

"*The Decency Code* is a much-needed antidote to the prevailing incivility we see in both the workplace and the nation. Harrison and Lukaszewski plot a practical approach to regain civility, integrity, and empathy in our relations with others. This is a must-read for leaders, investors, employees, and engaged citizens generally."

—HELIO FRED GARCIA,
President, Logos Consulting

"In *The Decency Code*, you will find a fully developed and actionable model for building a decent workplace culture. Anyone invested in building a corporate culture that inspires a sense of purpose, empowers human beings to do their best in any business climate, and inoculates their organizations from ethical failure will be well rewarded by applying the many lessons of this book. In their encouragement, humor, and compassion, Jim and Steve are committed to your success."

—RANJIT DE SOUSA,
President, Lee Hecht Harrison

THE
DECENCY
CODE

THE
DECENCY
CODE

THE LEADER'S PATH TO BUILDING INTEGRITY AND TRUST

STEVE HARRISON

JAMES E. LUKASZEWSKI

New York Chicago San Francisco Athens London Madrid
Mexico City Milan New Delhi Singapore Sydney Toronto

1 2 3 4 5 6 7 8 9 LCR 25 24 23 22 21 20

ISBN   978-1-260-45539-7
MHID   1-260-45539-4

e-ISBN   978-1-260-45540-3
e-MHID   1-260-45540-8

Library of Congress Control Number: 2020930266

McGraw-Hill Education books are available at special quantity discounts to use as premiums and sales promotions or for use in corporate training programs. To contact a representative, please visit the Contact Us pages at www.mhprofessional.com.

To Shirley Harrison, the love of my life for forty five years

*To our three kids: Amy, Leslie and Mark,
and our amazing grandchildren*

STEVE HARRISON

To Barbara Bray Lukaszewski, my sunshine girl for sixty years.

*To Shyloh Spurling who filled Barbara's final days
with joy, happiness, and friendship*

*To Debra Gelbach, Barbara's biographer, keeping her joy,
inspiration, and memories alive*

JAMES E. LUKASZEWSKI

CONTENTS

FOREWORD

All of us in the world of workforce transformation are continually challenged to find the best practices that will produce the outcomes worthy of great organizations. I have made a career out of helping business leaders transform their workforces so they can have an impact on the world. In the course of that work, I have witnessed many leaders struggle to achieve business success while maintaining the trust and respect of their colleagues. Building and maintaining trust and respect are among the most important work of leaders.

It helps to have a model. For me, Steve Harrison serves that role. I met Steve shortly after I joined Lee Hecht Harrison (also known as LHH). I found myself challenged by a demanding situation. One of our biggest clients had recently merged with another company, and leadership faced a number of challenges on the people side. It was clear to me that the client was looking for something more.

I asked Steve to spend some time with the client, and the results were magical. He offered a completely different perspective, shifting the frame of the situation from challenge to opportunity. The client came away from the interaction inspired.

I studied how Steve did it. I was immediately impressed by the daily behaviors Steve displayed from the moment we met. He modeled the practice, well described in this book, of greeting the receptionist as the CEO of First Impressions. He reminded me that in any relationship getting the first impression right has a durable impact on the long-term experience. Any business that values fashioning customer delight based on positive touch points understands this dynamic.

First impressions are telling. I have interviewed countless candidates for positions, and they are invariably agreeable and well-behaved. After the interview, I often ask the receptionist for their experience with the candidate. Candidate interaction with the front desk seems to me highly revealing of character. More than once, I have decided not to continue the conversation with a candidate because of what the receptionist reported.

Corporate leaders agree trust is paramount. Sustainable businesses are built on trust. Too often, however, the talk is little more than conceptual. This book demonstrates how organizations build trustworthy environments grounded in decencies. What has really shifted in today's business world is increased transparency. When a company breaks trust, the world knows about it immediately. A world driven by social media makes the whole topic of decency much more important than ever.

This book reminds us that repetition and recognition of small decencies are the two key elements of building resilient corporate cultures. If an organization focuses on the small things that need to be done every day, over time it will create the critical mass that yields the behavioral shifts we desire.

Steve and Jim Lukaszewski have joined up to write *The Decency Code*. America's Crisis Guru®, Jim brings four decades of experience assisting corporate leaders facing conflict, contention, controversy, or opposition. Steve's first book made me think about leadership dynamics in a new, bold way, and I predict that with Jim's contributions, *The Decency Code* will do the same for a new generation of readers by teaching them to take highly focused, civility- and decency-inspired, ethically appropriate action.

If you are genuinely invested in helping people without expectation of return, you are on the right track. In this book, Steve and Jim help you model leadership grounded in civilities and decencies and give you the tools to help integrate a culture of decencies into your organization. The resources they share will help you create a healthy management mindset, improve business performance, promote trust, reduce stress, and build better relationships with your colleagues and teammates.

I resonate with simple tools and concepts, often challenging to achieve. The concepts and tools that Steve and Jim share in *The Decency Code* may be straightforward and inexpensive to implement, but they require a resource that most enterprises find difficult to sustain: commitment over time. Sustaining a civil and decent culture—especially when an organization is stressed or struggling—is a measure of the resilience that every company needs to survive adversity.

One thing that sets Steve and Jim apart from other business authors is their compassion. They genuinely know the pressures that frontline supervisors, midlevel managers, and C-suite leaders face every day. In these pages, you will read of companies that have resisted unethical conduct as well as those that have succumbed. The book makes the case that a flourishing culture of civility and decency resists unethical conduct.

In *The Decency Code*, you will find a fully developed and actionable model for building a decent workplace culture. Anyone invested in building a corporate culture that inspires a sense of purpose, empowers human beings to do their best in any business climate, and inoculates their organizations from ethical failure will be well rewarded by applying the many lessons of this book. In their encouragement, humor, and compassion, Jim and Steve are committed to your success.

Ranjit de Sousa
President, Lee Hecht Harrison
Zurich, Switzerland

A WELCOME NOTE FROM THE AUTHORS

Why *The Decency Code* Will Matter to You

We'd like to take a moment to introduce you to *The Decency Code* and tell you why it will matter in your life. Why did you pick up this book, whether you're at a bookstore or you found in it in a library or someone shared it with you? We're guessing your questions are something like these five:

1. Can this book answer the questions I have, see, hear, or think about with respect to decency, civility, and integrity?
2. Can this book answer the questions that bother most of us about why there is such a decency denial and deficit in America and in the world today?
3. How do I bring my own personal views and decency, civility, and integrity habits from my personal and family life into my working and professional life?

4. How can I help reduce the contention and controversy that seems to grow everywhere?
5. Can this book help me and those I care about have happier lives and more satisfying careers?

The Decency Code is a book that answers these questions and much more.

Just take a dip into any chapter. We believe you will find some important answers and perhaps even more important questions that need to be answered as you learn more about *The Decency Code.*

In the past few years civility, integrity, and decency have been turned upside down and are now even more essential to discuss and explore. As we envisioned this book, beginning around 2009, we questioned ourselves with increasing intensity:

Why does any book about decency, civility, and integrity matter?

How is another book going to contribute to the growing public conversation of decency, civility, and integrity?

Can any book arm an individual against indecency, incivility, and phoniness?

As the book evolved, its purpose, value, and need became more evident to us as authors, and we hope it will for you too, as the reader, learner, and practitioner of *The Decency Code.*

Here are the perspectives we are coming from:

1. *The Decency Code* provides many pathways to respect, civility, and integrity. The most powerful pathways include accountability, civility, compassion, empathy, honesty, humility, and principle.
2. But there are even more pathways: apology, candor, character, destiny management (yours), dignity, empathy, engagement, forgiveness, honesty, openness, responsiveness, transparency, and truthfulness.
3. *The Decency Code* defines decency from different, relevant perspectives.
4. *The Decency Code* helps explain which barriers to decencies are hard to overcome: accountability vs. doing whatever it takes; civility vs. callousness and confrontation; compassion vs. indifference and suspicion; empathy vs. apathy and carelessness; honesty vs. culpability and silence; humility vs. arrogance and overbearance; and principle vs. insidious unethical behavior.
5. *The Decency Code* provides and provokes lessons you can apply to your daily life at work and home.
6. This is a book your boss can use (and you, if you're the boss) to move your organization more deeply into the concepts of civility, decency, and integrity, the three overriding components of *The Decency Code*.

Our goal for this book, and the conversations we hope it will trigger, is to answer these and other questions on every single page. As we wrote the book, our principal question was, "What questions does this page answer?" or "What questions on this page need to be answered?" or "What questions can only be answered by the reader, user, and practitioner of *The Decency Code*?"

We hope you'll join us.

Steve Harrison—New York

James E. Lukaszewski—Minneapolis
America's Crisis Guru®

January 2020

CHAPTER 1

WHY NOW?

> *"If we can't find a way to take an interest in our employees as people, we're committing them to a miserable work life, and that makes ships go a lot slower."*
> **—PATRICK LENCIONI**

The question this book will answer is, "Why is it that America has learned—better than any country or culture in the world—how to build great companies and great leaders to lead them, yet many of these same leaders seemingly look the other way as their companies and colleagues sink into ethical mischief and outright criminality?"

Why is it that even after the behavioral trauma of Enron, WorldCom, Tyco, Equifax, VW, Theranos, Madoff, Wells Fargo, Nissan, the beat goes on—seemingly unabated—fraud, bribery, insider trading rings, and Ponzi schemes remain ubiquitous.

And why is it that despite the Sarbanes-Oxley regulations, Dodd-Frank, and the growing ranks of compliance and risk officers, corporate roguishness and misbehavior persists among "leaders in loafers"?

This book proposes that the priority of rushing to greatness too often produces temporary perceptions of success and misguided leadership. All too frequently, it turns out that these great companies are not good companies, and their highly publicized and highly compensated leaders turn out to be compromised. Too many of these organizations and their leaders have been revealed to be unequal to the ethical standards to which they've committed. The authors prescribe a solution, one that may be shunned by some less enlightened corporate leaders but will become fully embraced by just about everybody else.

Our prescription is that the reporting of public companies as well as larger private companies needs to incorporate palpable evidence of their intentional ethic: developing and maintaining a civil culture; designing programs to promote the workplace as an ethical, desirable environment; rewarding values-based behavior, honesty, and integrity as much as profitability. In other words, organizations and leadership that can demonstrate that they are good companies with values that are so simple, sensible, constructive, helpful, and positive that only the critics, naysayers, and bellyachers will be opposed. After all, leadership is what drives decency, civility, integrity, and associated pathways that make up *The Decency Code*, including:

- Accountability
- Civility

- Compassion
- Empathy
- Honesty
- Humility
- Principle

Traditional media continue to swing between high treason and high glamour as they document the disconnect between corporate promises and leadership misbehavior. Film, TV, and print media often trade on the excessive lifestyles of those who rise and fall in the tainted glamour of the tarnished business rock star or big-time producer.

Consider two vivid examples of corporate shame. Volkswagen altered the pollution control devices on 800,000 vehicles to falsely meet environmental standards. Wells Fargo employees intentionally cheated millions of customers who found that their trust in the bank was betrayed by misaligned incentives established by flawed leadership. In both cases, employees and their supervisors and managers by the thousands were responding to their bosses' signals or incentives. The corporate cultures of the respective organizations rather than growing stronger were made weaker, then too weak to deter misbehavior. These are two real and unfolding stories of intentional bad, unethical, and some clearly illegal management behavior. When this book is published, there will likely be other instances of corporate misbehavior.

Decency Requires More
Than Compliance

Compliance and ethics programs are proliferating; business schools are expanding their curricula; ethics and engagement managers are being hired; and leadership programs are multiplying as the subject of corporate culture has become sexy. But the incidents of fraud and gross misconduct continue. The weekly TV series *American Greed* continues to report on stunning real-life examples of leadership misbehavior.

This book proposes that since corporate greed continues and since the post-Enron controls have been inadequate to detect, prevent, deter, or eliminate wrongdoing, different answers are needed if only because of the realities of the new world of work: flexible, insecure, robotic, delayered, virtual, unstable, out-of-balance, fast-moving, complex, ambiguous, global, diverse, and ruthlessly competitive. Members of Generation X, Generation Y, and Generation Z coexist with the survivors of what we term the "RE" generation in business, as companies REdeploy, REorganize, REfocus, REnew, REalign, and REengineer. Organizational change efforts have been described by management guru Tom Peters as upsizing, downsizing, rightsizing, and capsizing. To quote change management expert Charles Handy, "a work world of seemingly endless whitewater!"

We argue that institutionalized decency is a success factor in helping leaders and their workforces to REvitalize, REinvent, REinvest, and REspect. Now, a new kind of manager is needed: whitewater navigators who thrive in our turbulent work world. Leaders who understand that the antidote to corporate cultural disorder is leadership to help replace confusion with order, opaqueness with clarity, complexity with simplicity, hopelessness with confidence, greed with selflessness, and suspicion with trust.

The ongoing trust deficit is, in the eyes of one compliance expert, an unfortunate reality. Thus, he said, there are always people looking for shortcuts, intent on gaming the system, who in good times get greedy and in bad times get selfish. It has become clear that something more than regulation, jail terms, compliance training, hotlines, and values statements is needed. This book argues that the new age whitewater leader has tools at his or her disposal to forge an environment that will sustain an enabling culture where innovation is stimulated, performance is rewarded, trust is deep-rooted, and where it "feels good to be here." The indispensable element is trust.

The Lexicon of Trust Busters

During his 50-year career in crisis intervention and prevention, covering hundreds of assignments in the United States and globally, helping leaders and their organizations prepare for, respond to, survive, and recover from crises, Jim Lukaszewski has developed a lexicon of leadership trust-busters:

- Arrogance (executive pomposity)
- Testosterosis (hitting back first)
- Broken promises

- Fear-creation
- Deception
- Denial
- Overplaying strengths
- Lack of empathy
- Procrastination
- Disrespect
- Ducking responsibility
- Dismissiveness
- Disparagement
- Inauthenticity
- Concealment
- Lying
- Isolation/AWOL
- Intimidation
- Overoptimism
- Sarcasm
- Minimizing
- Tone deafness
- Corrosive delegation
- Misguided incentives
- Operating on the edge
- Fostering a "do whatever it takes" culture

They did what? Said what? Promised what? Now what? Any combination of these trust-busters can be corrosive to the human spirit and counterproductive to culture enrichment. Think Albert J. Dunlap at Sunbeam, Dennis Kozlowski at Tyco, Ken Lay at Enron, or Bernie Madoff.

They destroyed trust and created victims and critics, some of whom look for and find opportunities for revenge.

Rather, it's about integrity, compassion, truthfulness, transparency, apology, inclusiveness, and the morality of ethical expectations of leaders and leadership. Jim describes himself as more of a management pathologist. He has seen so much repetitive negative behavior, decision making, and self-forgiveness that he has developed insights into the pathologies—the origins, nature, and course of negative management behavior and of leaders who are headed for trouble.

Steve Harrison's 50-year career spans labor relations, human resources, entrepreneurship, and global corporate consultancy, including career transition (outplacement), leadership development, and employee engagement. Steve's observations align with Jim's as they relate to workplace instability and leadership shortcomings, especially in turbulent times. As well, they are aligned in proposing the antidotes:

- Telling the truth
- Listening
- Genuine recognition
- Keeping rich traditions
- Modeling ethical and compliant behavior
- Demonstrating a willingness to sacrifice profits for principle
- Developing and sustaining a coaching culture
- Building trust at every opportunity

- Respecting innovation failure
- Collaborating genuinely
- Vocalizing, publicizing, and operationalizing core values, ethical standards, civility, and decency—in all scheduled operations and performance reviews, in all group company functions, in every new-hire onboarding session, in every CEO message, in all compliance and ethics training, in all executive coaching programs, and in all leadership programs and talent development processes

What Decency Looks Like

A business decency is a thoughtful, meaningful gesture offered that in ways small and large can enhance a corporate culture. Decencies are how we more humanely treat one another. John Cowan, author of *Small Decencies*, reminds us that we can be true to our values both at home and at work. The more humanely we treat one another, the better we will be as people and the better we will be in doing our life's work.

We are colleagues who want to make a positive difference in another person's day. Out of such actions, multiplied dozens of times over a period, corporate cultures are enriched and ethical behavior reinforced. Widely accepted and adopted, decencies become a force multiplier for employee engagement.

The late Herb Kelleher understood this when he created Southwest Airlines' "culture committee" to honor people in unglamorous jobs: "top wrench award" or "top cleaner award." Doug Conant, Campbell's ex-CEO, regularly handwrote thank-you notes to deserving employees all over the world. Herbert Baum, ex-CEO of Dial Corporation, regularly held informal chats—serving hot dogs—as he hosted "Hot Dogs with Herb."

Tim Cook, CEO of Apple, was inspired in 2017 to initiate a national conversation about the moral responsibilities of businesses. Jim Lukaszewski has taken Tim Cook's commencement address at MIT on June 9, 2017, and transformed it into Lukaszewski's "Civility and Decency Manifesto." Highlights of Jim's manifesto include:

- Business has a moral obligation greater than the accumulation of wealth and sole allegiance to Wall Street.
- Businesses should be places where individuals can find meaning, purpose, and can serve humanity . . . something greater than themselves.
- Businesses, like technology, can do great things. But like technology, businesses don't necessarily want to do great things, they just do things. Business purpose comes from those who lead.
- Keeping people at the center of business and in life can have enormous impact.
- Whatever you do in life it must be infused with the humanity, values, and decency that each of us is born with.
- Use technology to reinforce and amplify the rules of decency and avoid pettiness and negativity.

- Measure your impact on humanity by the lives you touch, rather than popularity.
- Stay on your personal course, focused on what really matters.
- Bring your values, compassion, empathy, and concern for consequences into your daily life and your work. Avoid those who advise otherwise.
- When you know your course is right, have the courage to take a stand.
- When you see a problem or an injustice, recognize that you are the only one to fix it.
- Use your mind and hands and heart to build something bigger than yourself.
- Strive to create the best, give the best, do the best for everyone.

We applaud Tim Cook's real vision. His vision lays a useful groundwork for this book. His passion and his quest for a fraud-free business culture reinforces the authors' experienced and deeply held conviction that the terms "integrity," "ethics," and "values" are too theoretical and intangible to be clear, vivid, and actionable for corporate cultures and their leaders in turbulent times. The power of institutionalized, tangible, visible, measurable, and pervasive decencies creates a deterrent to misbehavior, misdeeds, and contaminants to employee engagement. Cultural decency helps inoculate workplaces from the "doing whatever it takes" crowd, regardless of consequences.

Whitewater Leaders

The coauthors argue that the keys to whitewater leadership effectiveness include agility, adaptability, and intuition. We are familiar with the seemingly endless variety in leadership theory: authoritative, collaborative, servant, charismatic, emotionally intelligent, level-5, "blue ocean," etc. But successful "whitewater navigators," regardless of their predominant leadership styles, display a unique talent, *especially in a crisis*: the ability and agility to adopt and embody most of these styles during any given day. Collaborators need to be decisive; authoritarians need to be collaborative; quiet and humble leaders need to step up and communicate more aggressively than they ever have; noisy leaders need to know when to "zip it up"; cerebral or process-oriented leaders quickly learn that turbulent times place a premium on managing decisively.

And ironically, during the very time when they're reacting, the effective whitewater leader needs to anticipate, to "see around corners," in the words of Colin Powell. As one CEO said, "I spend half my day thinking: What am I not thinking of? What could possibly catch me by surprise?"

In 1982, Terrence Deal and Allan Kennedy published their groundbreaking book *Corporate Cultures*. They said this: "Great leaders . . . make success attainable and human. And the great stories that emerge in a culture tend to spread information about valued behavior." We believe that valued behavior includes a universal commitment to small decencies—gestures by leaders that are tangible, replicable, and sustainable. They create stories . . . and stories travel:

- Praising people in public, criticizing in private[1]
- Greeting visitors promptly and enthusiastically
- Valuing receptionists—they are our Directors of First Impressions
- Rejecting executive pomposity
- Promoting trust through accessibility, transparency, and candor
- Institutionalizing civility
- Making a difference!

Institutions Laid Low

When our institutions are laid low, it's often because of internal events and intentionally counterproductive decisions of leadership. Think of Volkswagen in the wake of a systematic effort to cheat on emissions tests. Such events—ethical shortcuts, fraud, deception, misrepresentations—are invariably self-imposed internal episodes that arise because people are fallible and incentives are perverse.

This book focuses on the challenges imposed from within. These are the activities that are covered by the newspapers and cable TV shows. They lead to resignations and firings, payments of huge fines, and, occasionally, criminal charges. These behaviors violate well-understood ethical, cultural, and legal norms. The violations create extraordinary challenges for leaders, many of whom fail to rise to the challenge. These violations are always a choice. Collectively we call them "incivilities." Decency is the antidote. Decency is also a choice.

The Decency Code is about promoting one choice over the other. Think of this book as your guide to structured decency in the workplace and beyond. We believe that decency scaled up to an institutional level is fundamental to corporate success in a globalizing world. Yet it is no secret that many of our institutions seem more devoid of decencies than ever.

Building Resilience

The focus of this book is about building resiliency against corporate misconduct and disengagement. We consider the causes, patterns, prevention, and deterrence of indecency. We look at what options companies have for deterring, preventing, detecting, and exposing incivilities.

As long as organizations must recruit from the human race, incivility seems inevitable. But it's certainly possible to prevent many indecencies, detect them early, expose them to the light of day, and minimize their frequency and cost. A corporate culture committed to decency represents the most powerful inoculation against indecency. When decencies triumph over incivility, a superior level of employee engagement results. This book makes a case for integrating decency and integrity into our work and private lives.

Decency starts with a commitment to verbal and written communication that is predominantly positive and carries messages that are sensible, constructive, positive, helpful, empathetic, and ethical and benefit the recipient of the message more than the sender—what Jim Lukaszewski refers to as The Ingredients of Leadership. A culture that is based on greed, opportunism, and exploiting unearned advantage leads to incivility, promotes deception, and frustrates mitigation and resolution.

Decency often keeps leaders in crisis from making the worst possible mistake: the cover-up. History shows that the cover-up is almost always considered a greater betrayal than the underlying crime. Decency reminds leaders that, in the end, it's not what you do that matters most, but what you do about what you did.

How Do These Two Authors Find Themselves in the Same Book?

We'd like to share a few words about the authors, how they met, and why their complementary skills are perfect for a book called *The Decency Code*.

Steve Harrison is the author of *The Manager's Book of Decencies: How Small Gestures Build Great Companies*. He serves as chairman of Lee Hecht Harrison, the largest career transition and talent management firm in the world, with 400 offices in 60 countries. He has spent his career promoting the lasting power of decency to engage employees and build enabling corporate cultures.

The focus of James E. Lukaszewski (Loo-ka-SHEV-skee) is cultural incivility and all the ways that organizations sabotage themselves. Jim's most recent book is *Lukaszewski on Crisis Communication: What Your CEO Needs to Know About Reputation Risk and Crisis Management.* It is widely considered the bible of crisis management. Many executives throughout the land have Jim Lukaszewski on speed dial. Known throughout the country as America's Crisis Guru®, Jim is respected for his ability to help executives look at problems from a variety of sensible, constructive, and principled perspectives. When there is a scandal or trouble brewing in corporate America, Jim's phone usually rings. Think of a major corporate scandal, and chances are good that Jim was recruited to mitigate the problem. But Jim's most powerful work is represented by corporate scandals you never heard of because they were resolved quickly or prevented altogether.

The worlds of the authors converged about 25 years ago when Steve Harrison's company experienced an isolated but embarrassing scandal that was featured in the *Wall Street Journal.* It was a crisis that required the best response. Steve was referred to Jim Lukaszewski for help in resolving the issues created by the unethical behavior of an employee. The results of that engagement cemented a powerful professional and personal relationship between the two men.

What's fascinating about it is the two different worlds Jim and Steve have occupied all these years. The reader may find it helpful to understand the common and contrasting views of the two authors.

Steve: his fundamental philosophy is that the vast majority of firms in the US and likely other countries and cultures operate within the parameters of being useful, helpful, productive organizations. Each, through its business operations, provides productive employment and opportunities to grow personally and professionally and, to varying degrees, is a reasonable place to work.

Jim's fundamental philosophy comes from an entirely different perspective, studying the pathology of management and leadership misbehavior observed over 40 years. He used this knowledge in real time to guide the recovery of 300 companies, domestic and international, through more than 400 victim-producing events. Lukaszewski believes that while every organization experiences a variety of difficulties and challenges as it operates, those that suffer serious adverse circumstances do so as the result of their intentional decisions, acts, and omissions. A leader decides to cross a line, deliberately ignoring existing regulatory controls, rules, and cultural norms. Jim's client companies experience self-inflicted, extraordinarily stressful, victim-producing events. The pathology of these circumstances results from intentionally inappropriate or unlawful behavior and management bungling.

It's a relatively small universe, but one that produces devastating and often highly visible negative results. He

maintains that despite the protestations of troubled organizations and cultures and their misbehaving leadership,
the choices between ethical decision making and unethical
decision making are always clear and always intentional.

How the Book Is Organized

The Decency Code charts multiple paths to decency and
integrity. The Foreword, by Ranjit de Sousa, president of
Lee Hecht Harrison, expresses the need for decencies and
civility in today's workplaces. Following the welcome note
from the authors, Chapter 1 makes the case for having the
Decency Code. Chapter 2 shows how corporate culture
and employee engagement are influenced by a commitment to decency and civility.

Chapters 3 through 6 make the case for decencies
as a business imperative. Chapter 3 defines the concept.
Chapter 4 presents a rationale for decency as not just a
nice-to-have but, in fact, an indispensable element for any
organization that aspires to excellence. Chapter 5 describes
the elements of decency in operational terms. Chapter 6
describes real-world examples of how decencies are contagious and serve as force multipliers of ethical behavior.

Chapter 7 connects the dots between decency and
employee engagement. Most organizations are making
extensive investments in motivating their employees. This
chapter shows how decency is an essential component of
any employee engagement agenda.

There is no more critical time for decencies than when faithful employees, through no fault of their own, must be terminated. Chapter 8 describes decencies when separating employees. Terminating managers will find time-tested practices for not only supporting separated employees during this difficult period but also providing critical information to surviving employees.

Chapter 9 summarizes the role of decencies in creating a resilient corporate culture by considering the ethical expectations for leaders by those they lead. "A Closing Perspective from the Authors" concludes the book by presenting a map to help today's organizations move from business as usual to becoming workplaces of decency and engagement.

We are glad you are on this journey to decency in the workplace and beyond. Let's get started.

CHAPTER 2

CORPORATE CULTURE AND EMPLOYEE ENGAGEMENT

> *"Everyone's reputation is made on a daily basis. There are little incremental things—worthwhile efforts, moments you were helpful to others—and after a lifetime, they can add up to something."*
>
> **—CHESLEY B. "SULLY" SULLENBERGER**

Passengers on a delayed Air Canada flight were frustrated. Air Canada Flight 608 left Toronto on March 5, 2019, on its way to Halifax, Nova Scotia. But poor weather in Halifax closed the airport, so Flight 608 was diverted to a small airport in Fredericton, where its passengers ended up sitting on the tarmac for more than four hours. There was a snowstorm, it was late, and other planes occupied all the gates. The passengers were cold and hungry. As the plane languished on the runway, unable to get to a gate, the passengers became restless. There was no food on the plane, little water, less information. The flight attendants apologized that there was simply "nothing we can do."

Then the Air Canada pilot made a phone call. He knew that Minglers Restaurant and Pub in Oromocto might be open. It was. The pilot ordered 23 large pizzas. Despite the late hour and the fact that there were only three staff members on duty, the staff quickly prepared the cheese and pepperoni pizzas and delivered them right to the door of the stranded airplane. By that point the passengers on the Airbus 320 had been on the plane for eight hours.

You can call that good customer service. We call it an example of decency at work and exquisitely fine-tuned employee engagement. The pilot is a poster child for corporate decency. In the face of institutional inertia—"We're sorry, there's simply nothing we can do"—the pilot made a phone call. He didn't ask for permission or make a big deal of it. He looked at the situation and acted.

For the Sake of Decency

This book is all about extending ourselves for the sake of decency. Decency nourishes what is best in our organizations. It's not just good on an individual or team level, it promotes a culture that reinforces core values and helps inoculate the organization from misbehavior.

A theme of this book is that organizational success is not a permanent condition. It must be cultivated at every level. Success is a fluid and ever-changing state that requires continuous care and nourishment. Our organizations often generate high-minded statements of principles and values. That's not the hard part. It's easy to hold out principles when conditions are ideal. The hard part is sustaining those principles and values on a day-to-day basis, frequently against a backdrop of business threats and scarce resources. The practice of decency as described in this book is part of any organization's commitment to reflexively modeling those principles and values when the going gets tough.

Decency is all about caring.

Caring, like decency, is a fragile thing. Loss of caring happens incrementally. The pattern unfolds through a series of small choices. Seemingly inoffensive compromises to ethical business practices, treating employees fairly, customer service, or product quality lead to a gradual disintegration of decency, leading to mediocrity or worse by a thousand cuts. In the airline industry, for example, baggage was transported free for the first 75 years. Following airline deregulation in the 1970s, airlines began finding ways to recover the revenue lost through competition. Charging for baggage delivered $9 billion in cost-free revenue.

The trend in this industry is negative. Mindless, careless, and insensitive decisions like redesigning planes with smaller aisles and smaller seats, when clearly the data shows body size is increasing is just one example. This simply sends the wrong signals.

When intentional misbehavior moves beyond simple negative irritations and discomforts and moves into operations, catastrophe can be the result. Case in point is the current grounding of all Boeing 737 MAX aircraft following two crashes in the first few months of this new aircraft's operation, killing hundreds of people. The planes remain grounded because investigations indicate reduction in safety procedures—software problems that were ignored. As this book goes to press the evidence of intentional malfeasance, cutting corners, and ignoring warnings from employees, including their chief pilot, requires that the 737 MAX aircraft remain grounded until every problem is found and fixed and this is confirmed by independent, outside aircraft experts.

The incremental abandonment of organizational ideals, principles, and values delivers toxic blows, and companies practicing these behaviors find themselves in ethical, legal, or reputational jeopardy. We've seen the degradation of organizational ideals in businesses and institutions of all kinds. When people and organizations veer away from the core principles that enabled their success, they enter treacherous waters that can lead to their undoing.

Employee Engagement Starts When Management Supports Employees' Daily Goals

Among culture-conscious employers, employee engagement is a hot topic. Hot? A better word is scorching, and for good reason. Employee engagement is a critical component of attracting and retaining talent. Turnover is usually bad news for an organization. It's bad for teamwork and productivity. It destroys morale, degrades innovation, and weakens organizational trust. Most of all, turnover represents an unnecessary expense as the organization commits precious resources to replacing employees.

There are a variety of engagement strategies organizations can take. Some of these can be elaborate and require significant training and a budget. But employee engagement requires neither a large budget nor a magic formula or gimmicks. What's required first and foremost is management's recognition that employees determine their engagement based on personal values and concerns, rather than what's best from the company's or organization's point of view. This stems from the failure of management to recognize that the more tenured leaders become, the more their life is defined by their work and work goals. Employees, on the other hand, even those most senior, tend to determine how engaged they'll become based on the positive impact of their experiences at work and the way their work contributes to their self-esteem, personal goals, and family life.

Decency-driven engagement practices are usually available at low or no cost. Engagement practices that flow out of an organizational culture committed to decency can be powerful tools to counter the problems of employee turnover and tune-out. They also serve as a viable strategy for greatly improving workplace experiences with employees who stay.

The dichotomy between employee needs and management's erroneous assumptions about those needs, put starkly, is that many employees' primary goal for their workday is to get home on time. Management's primary goal for their workday is getting the work done, no matter how long they have to stay to do it. This is the conundrum of employee engagement.

It's All About Engagement

Leaders have an amplified role in the employee engagement process because of their position as "chief culture officers." Done right, an engaged, values-driven culture can signal a relentless commitment to quality of working life and a connection between work and home.

Integral to ensuring an enabling culture is institutionalized decency, a tightly woven, leadership-driven, relentless pursuit of civility, transparency, trust, integrity, and unified purpose. Codes of conduct are helpful if they're brought to life. Values statements are helpful if they're brought to life. Ethics and compliance manuals are essential if they're brought to life. Simply, understandably, repeatedly, constructively.

Cynicism in the workplace is as widespread today as in the past. Employees—including executives—are checking out too often, phoning it in, or in some cases undermining the organization. This cynicism is often related to excessive profits, needless losses, or macroeconomic conditions that could have been anticipated.

A stunning symptom of this reality is the stagnant state of employee engagement. The Gallup Organization has researched millions of employees in hundreds of US organizations. According to the most recent "State of the American Workforce" report, 85 percent of employees are not engaged or are actively disengaged at work.[1] Look at it another way: If a department has 20 employees, only 3 people on the payroll are giving it their all. The rest are phoning it in.

The impacts and economic consequences of this global engagement pattern represent $7 trillion in lost productivity according to Gallup's "State of the Global Workplace" report. Eighteen percent of workers are actively disengaged in their work and workplace, while 67 percent are "not engaged." These are not a company's laggards or worst performers, the report insists. They are simply—or not so simply—indifferent to the goals of the organization. They grudgingly exchange their time for a paycheck, but they withhold their best ideas and creativity. It's a global engagement pattern that may underscore how poorly performance is managed.

Many well-intentioned programs designed to address the problem of engagement are misfiring. The new workforce is looking for access to information, advance warning of adverse developments, more of a voice in decision making, and ways to connect their home life to their working life. They see work and life as interconnected, and they want their job to be a part of their identity.

Employee engagement is essential to organizational success, yet many companies struggle with inspiring and positively challenging their workforces to go above and beyond. When we get performance management right, engagement will naturally rise. And the potential impact on the bottom line is significant. The best organizations achieve earnings per share growth that is more than four times that of their competitors, according to a 2017 report from Gallup.[2]

There can be little doubt of the critical role employee engagement plays in the success of work teams, departments, enterprises, and even entire economies. In the United States alone, disengaged employees cost organizations an estimated $450 to $550 billion each year, according to Gallup.[3]

More Engaged Leaders

The key to more engaged workers is more engaged and trustworthy leaders. Employees see right through initiatives that are basically little more than manipulation. No one wants to feel manipulated, especially by leaders who are seen as uncaring and aloof. In his book *The Meaning Revolution*, Fred Kofman asks, "If engagement is so crucial to an organization's performance, and if the strategies to produce it are so simple, why aren't there more engaging leaders, and why aren't more companies dramatically increasing employee engagement?"

McKinsey and Company routinely asks executives what they found most often missing in creating a peak performance environment. The response: a strong sense of meaning, without which employees quickly disengage and see their work not as a career but as just a job.

Employee engagement doesn't necessarily respond to promotions that can seem designed to increase sales, reduce costs, build market share, or grow shareholder value. All these goals are important, but even if an organization achieves them, it can still suffer if employee engagement does not keep pace. Personal engagement is required for organizational success. Engagement produces group cohesion, solidarity, trust, mutual respect, and an environment in which people can work together to accomplish audacious goals.

Bolt-On Engagement

It's futile for companies to simply throw money at conventional employee engagement initiatives and think that will solve the problem. These bolt-on functions typically let companies check the right boxes while they continue to engage in practices inconsistent with the values and initiatives they evangelize. Similarly, establishing a standalone employee engagement function, without integrating it into every corner of the organization, does little to create a culture that infuses processes with values, catalyzes ethical behavior, and holds all stakeholders—including leaders—accountable.

We recently visited a Fortune 500 company that had a celebrated ethics statement prominently displayed on the walls. The ethics statement was also printed on the back of the security badges every employee wore on lanyards around their necks. At a private lunch with some employees, we asked about whether the ethics statement actually catalyzed the company to act more ethically. One of the employees looked sad and reported the following:

> Just a month ago, the company promoted a manager to a senior executive position. He received a corner office, more money, a big bonus, stock options, company car, the whole package. He got the promotion because he tripled his quota. He achieved that feat while violating every single one of the values we say we stand for. So, you tell me. Should we pay attention to these values, or should we pay attention to what actually gets rewarded around here?

As we left that luncheon, the employee was sadly reading the words on the back of the lanyard around his neck. We couldn't help thinking that the violated values of that posted statement were more of a weight around his neck than an inspiration. The takeaway is that employee engagement is a matter of alignment. If a bank (think Wells Fargo) proclaims, "We value what's right for our customers in everything we do," but then tolerates and even encourages workers to open unwanted accounts for customers without their knowledge, the values become a source of derision, not a set of guiding principles.

Values on the Wall

Sadly, this episode is more often the rule than the exception. Too many leaders focus more on articulating their organization's mission and values than on living up to those values. More than 70 percent of all S&P 500 companies promote integrity as a core value, according to an analysis by finance professors Luigi Guiso, Paola Sapienza, and Luigi Zingales.[4] The researchers wanted to determine how advertised values correlated with financial performance. In a follow-up study of 679 US companies and more than 400,000 employees, the same researchers concluded that "companies that lived their values in practice achieved higher productivity, higher profitability, and an increased ability to attract talent compared with those that did not."[5] Integration moves the "values on the wall" to "values in action."

Corporate culture consists of the sacred values, attitudes, behaviors, standards, beliefs, traditions, and ritual moments that define an organization as it is lived. Culture is embedded in the stories we tell one another about ourselves in an attempt to make ongoing sense of why we do what we do. What matters most is how leaders behave. It's all about authenticity and alignment.

What we propose in *The Decency Code* is that in a workplace that is diverse, competitive, global, and virtual, the ultimate measure of effectiveness is whether the words match the music, and if not, what leadership proposes to do about it. Our main point is that what leaders can do to make a difference in employee engagement is inject their cultures with *everyday acts of decency* that may represent only 2 percent of what they do, but 98 percent of who they are.

Institutionalized Decencies

Our book is about the potentially powerful cultural impact of institutionalized decencies. Recent frequent conversations around the impact of greater decency, civility, and ethics are significant but too conceptual to drive the point home in the workplace. However, think of the nightly news stories reporting real-life examples of decency: storm- or fire-related selfless acts of sacrifice and bravery—the vivid, indelible, three-dimensional images that can set examples for future behavior. These are much more compelling than statistics around burnt forest acreage. They have the enduring effect of engaging the audience. Helicopter rescues, rooftop survival, pet rescues, nursing home evacuations all make memories and leave us with role models and, in some cases, even heroes.

In corporate cultures, it's vivid, actual examples of leadership selflessness, courage, generosity, collaboration, and even tough love that provide the elusive "glue" that's the essence of real, enduring employee engagement. An organization's culture becomes lasting, palpable, believable, and productive if it is bonded relentlessly to engagement activities: in recruitment, onboarding, orientation, leadership development, career development, operations reviews, performance reviews, talent management, conferences, training, and yes, even terminations. David Noer, noted consultant and author of *Healing the Wounds: Overcoming the Trauma of Layoffs and Revitalizing Downsized Organizations*, created the following recipe for "cultural glue":

- *Fill glue pot with the fresh, pure, clear water of undiluted human spirit.*
- *Take special care not to contaminate with preconceived ideas or to pollute with excess control.*
- *Fill slowly; notice that the pot only fills from the bottom up. It's impossible to fill it from the top down.*
- *Stir in equal parts of customer focus and pride in good work.*
- *Bring to a boil and blend in a liberal portion of diversity; one-part self-esteem and one-part tolerance.*
- *Fold in accountability.*
- *Simmer until smooth and thick, stirring with shared leadership and clear goals.*
- *Season with a dash of humor and a pinch of adventure.*
- *Let cool, then garnish with a topping of core values.*
- *Serve by coating all boxes in the organization chart with particular attention to the white spaces. With proper application, the boxes disappear and all that can be seen is productivity, creativity, and customer service.[6]*

Sculpting Fog

Central to today's discourse around corporate cultures is the issue of virtuality. How do you lead people you don't see and who don't see you? How do you operationalize Tom Peters's compelling advocacy of MBWA (management by walking around) in an operationally diffuse, increasingly remote workplace? Isn't the real leadership challenge about "sculpting fog" in a work world characterized not only by virtuality, but by job-sharing, contingent employment, portfolio careering, and in-betweening? In other words, where empowerment and career self-sufficiency rule?

Current and future leaders will be increasingly challenged by the trend toward telecommuting. Global Workplace Analytics claimed that 40 percent more US employers were offering flexible workplace options than five years ago.[7] Surveys show that upward of 80 percent of the US workforce would prefer to telework at least part of the time, according to Gallup's State of the American Workforce Report.[8]

Employee engagement strategies are now challenged by this new, mobile, virtual, and amorphous world of work. Cultivating engaged employees when they are in the same physical location is difficult enough. Building engagement with employees who work remotely adds extra layers of complexity and requires innovative ways to increase communication, collaboration, and community. Fortunately, the same technology that makes remote work possible provides opportunities to create a sense of shared purpose. Those technologies include robust videoconferencing, chat programs, and gamification.

The Birth of Employee Engagement

The engagement movement likely had its origin in the studies decades ago around morale, especially among returning World War II veterans and then factory production lines. The term "employee engagement" was coined in 1990 by Professor William Kahn of Boston University in a paper titled "Psychological Conditions of Personal Engagement and Disengagement at Work." While now universally accepted as an essential component of a sound corporate culture, it's still hard to pin down exactly what the term means. The Conference Board is helpful here. It defines employee engagement as "a heightened emotional connection that an employee feels for his or her organization that influences him or her to exert greater discretionary effort in his or her work."[9]

In other words, it's about the working environmental attributes that motivate employees to enthusiastically go above and beyond what's expected. "The emotional commitment the employee has to the organization and its goals," is a definition offered by *Forbes*.[10] Regardless of the definition, employee engagement turns out to be perhaps the most challenging success factor for any organization.

Early commentators on the subject were convinced that "keeping people" is in no small way a function of employer-sponsored benefits and perks. These are just a partial list of institutional perks intended to promote retention:

- Education assistance
- Casual dress policy
- Bring children to work days
- Flexible work schedules
- Free food
- Health/fitness facilities
- Relaxation zones
- Laundry/dry-cleaning services
- Mentoring programs
- Stock ownership
- Family outings
- Formal awards/recognition programs
- Community service days
- Telecommuting flexibility
- Leadership development

These perks are institutional in that, unlike small decencies, most need a budget and policy. Some of these programs have proved more effective than others. Engagement advocates argue, however, that it's the total working environmental attributes that motivate employees to go above and beyond what's expected. We would add it's the corporate cultural characteristics and leadership essentials that can make fraud and gross misconduct a remote consideration. So, employee engagement theory is less about happiness and more about quality of work life, ethical work life, values-driven work life.

Means to the End

Our book argues that employee engagement is a means to the end. A company must function excellently in other dimensions, too. If the other business tools are not in place, a team of supercharged, engaged employees who think they're working for a great company could one day arrive at work and find the gates chained. You could have low-performing businesses with highly engaged employees.

A recent IBM study of more than a million employees concluded that, ultimately, engagement happens one employee at a time, one interaction at a time.[11] It is this reality that, in aggregate, makes the case for a genuine commitment to decency in corporate culture. It's about one spontaneous gesture at a time. Sewn together, these gestures can form a tapestry of cultural richness, worthwhile traditions, priceless stories, and, ultimately, engaged colleagues.

Employee engagement has joined the litany of business fads—think MBO (management by objectives) or ZBB (zero-based budgeting)—that make their way around the corporate ecosystem and are often then jettisoned in favor of the NBT (next big thing). We are warned to be cautious of the "fashionality" of employee engagement.

Employee engagement can drive a more disciplined business strategy.

The Gallup organization has captured what workers say they want from an organization. Engaged employees want to know that their leaders:

- Think about me
- Know me
- Care about me
- Hear me
- Help me feel proud
- Help me review my contributions
- Help me grow
- Help me build mutual trust
- Challenge me[12]

The PwC authors of *Closing the Engagement Gap* put it even more succinctly in advising employers to:

- Know them
- Grow them
- Inspire them
- Involve them
- Reward them[13]

"U.S. workers have a trust problem," suggests a recent *Wall Street Journal* article by Lauren Weber. "Only about half of U.S. workers feel their employers are up front with them according to a survey about work and well-being by the

American Psychological Association" she writes. "And one quarter of Americans say they simply don't trust the companies they work for."[14]

Empathic Leaders Inspire Engagement

At one time, perhaps, employees were satisfied simply working for an organization with quality products or services that created satisfied customers. Somehow, we doubt it. We believe that in all periods, employees have sought a sense of engagement with their fellow workers and employers. Today, the bar has been raised. Employees demand to be partners in the goodwill that comes from serving customers well. In addition, they want the companies for which they work to do some social good along the way and stand for values beyond profit.

This is the essence of the challenge of employee engagement. Of course, employees want everything they have always wanted. They want a decent salary, decent working conditions, effective supervision, and a path toward development. And without sacrificing any of these, employees insist on jobs that give them a sense of purpose in a company they feel is making the world just a little better. As well, engagement extends to customers and other stakeholders.

Customers, for example, want to engage with products that not only satisfy them but respond to a real need and are offered at a fair price. But customers and investors also want to associate with organizations that stand for decent values and leverage those values with actionable practices in such areas as gender equity, diversity, and environmental sustainability. Stakeholders want to associate with companies that are viewed as force multipliers for the social issues that the stakeholders see as most important. In short, stakeholders increasingly value social impact.

Supporter or Cynic

Whether you're a supporter or cynic about employee engagement, the issue will not disappear. One reason is the justifiable concern among hiring authorities about talent shortages. Over the years, creative initiatives aimed at strengthening employee engagement have been well intended, but their sustainability has been challenged. Most important is the degree to which employee engagement is a factor in creating or at least reinforcing an ethical culture. The Ethics Resource Center in 2010 asked two key questions:

1. Does ethical culture play a part in employee engagement?
2. Does management's commitment to ethics impact employees' engagement with the company as a whole?[15]

The findings:

- Management's commitment to ethics is particularly important for employee engagement.

- Employees who already felt engaged were less likely to feel pressure to commit misconduct.
- Engaged employees are more likely to report misconduct when they witness it, thus reducing the company's ethics risk.
- A positive impression of the company's ethical culture promotes employee engagement, while misconduct erases it.

Philosophy of Doing Business

There is a philosophy of doing business that goes beyond the transfer of goods and services. It calls for an infusion of values in the form of small decencies—business gestures that are cost-free or nearly so and can make a firm a more effective and supportive place to work. They can be implemented without a lot of planning or training. And they are invariably focused on customers or employees.

Everyone in your organization can model decency. You have permission. You have the resources. What you need to do is act. A company's culture can be molded—for the better—by the cumulative power of small decencies. It's about the way leaders choose to behave—the actions leaders embrace—every day, especially during the quiet moments when we think no one is watching.

Employee engagement is the critical success factor that often distinguishes the most successful organization from the runners-up. Employee engagement is less about what's missing and much, much more about the resources that are available. The most effective way to build employee engagement is through a coordinated set of decencies: individual gestures that help define the larger environment, build the foundation of an ethical culture, and help inoculate the culture against gross misconduct that violates ethical norms. Corporate leaders can post ethics statements, but buy-in is a decision that each individual employee makes every day. The government can require compliance with regulations, but it cannot legislate ethics, values, and civility.

Integrity needs to be cultivated and supported through shared values and enforced norms. Integrity needs to be perfected through day-to-day practice. Integrity is a constant, whatever the situation. What we have is the opportunity to uphold promises and fulfill duties in every situation that faces us, large and small. Integrity is also about a practice and a habit of keeping promises, the ones we make explicitly and the ones that are implied in all our relationships.

We confront a time when the theme of indecency and incivility is increasing in our workplaces, our institutions, and our personal relationships. But by recognizing and resisting the ways we tend to squander trust in our lives at work and at home, we can repair the disconnects that create vulnerabilities in our institutions. *The Decency Code* exposes how too often our culture sanctions breaches of integrity large and small through an array of rationalizations and euphemisms.

Leaders will never realize their full potential until they help people contribute to their full potential. Employees today deserve to contribute in an environment that allows them to liberate their full potential. Leaders today can help the people they serve experience an entirely different level of engagement at work. It begins when we create the conditions in which they willingly bring more of themselves to work.

The return on engagement can be significant. Evidence shows that sales, profits, innovation, customer satisfaction, and every other key metric is positively impacted by how much employees care. When you raise employee levels of engagement, you've overcome a significant barrier to superior performance.

CHAPTER 3

DECENCIES: A WORKING DEFINITION

> *"Enlightened managers know that serving and supporting unleashes much more energy, talent, and commitment than commanding and controlling."*
>
> **—KOUZES AND POSNER, *The Indian Journal of Public Administration***

All of us, at one time or another, have used the word *decency* in some form. We may associate decency with being considerate, courteous, gracious, honest, honorable, thoughtful, appropriate, tasteful, respectful, obliging, or helpful. We talk of decent acts, decent behaviors, a decent person, a decent wage. We find ourselves relating to a word that reflects specific behaviors. Even the opposite, *indecent*, is something that most of us can relate to: "indecent exposure" is quite vivid to us. "Are you decent?" was originally backstage theater jargon for "Are you dressed?"

Let's narrow down the definition of a business decency. A business decency is a gesture offered without expectation of reward that, in ways small and large, can change the corporate culture for the better. This definition may be a bit dense, so let's unpack it term by term.

A decency is, first, a *discrete gesture* or action. A decency must be acted out for it to have meaning. Decency can't be suggested; it must be acted. Good intentions remain intentions until there is visible follow-through. Wanting to be decent is like wanting to lose weight. "I want to be decent" has as much to do with actually being decent as "I want to lose weight" has to do with actually doing the work of losing weight.

A genuine decency is *freely offered* rather than compelled. A decency cannot be coerced by a supervisor or required by a published policy. It is voluntary or spontaneous on the part of the individual offering it because, in this instance, it is consistent with the individual's—and, hopefully, the organization's—values. Providing employees with safe working conditions is not, by the definition of this book, a decency; it's just the minimum requirement for being safe in business. Whenever something is codified by such bodies as the US Occupational Safety and Health Administration (OSHA), it is an obligation rather than a decency.

An equal opportunity workplace free of harassment is a requirement rather than a decency; it's an expectation that has become the desired norm and is enforced by the rule of law. While the continuum between decencies and mandates is always evolving, what's important is that at the time the small decency gesture is made, the giver is acting in the best interest of someone else of his or her own volition with zero expectation of reward.

If you offer a gesture with the expectation of explicit reciprocity, it becomes a transaction, a form of barter. There is nothing wrong with this; the vast bulk of human interactions operate on this basis. "I'll help you cut your lawn if you help me build my fence." A gesture, however decent, offered to advance an ulterior motive, however beneficial, is not a decency, but a bribe. Having an ulterior or hidden motive negates the decency. People can usually smell a hidden agenda a mile away, and when they do, they run, not walk, the other way.

The terms *decency* and *civility* are related, and we use both terms in this book. Civility is formal politeness and courtesy in behavior or speech and, as such, is a subset of decency. Civility is a good thing to display, but decency, we suggest, goes deeper. A leader can be thoroughly unscrupulous and still be civil. Decency invokes matters of character and values. A leader may be civil and still be toxic.

Decencies Are Transformational

The unilateral and spontaneous quality of decencies make them powerful and often transformational. For that reason, decencies are no longer merely transactional; they become transformational. They have the ability to transform both the giver and the receiver and affect the culture at the same time. Decencies often catalyze powerful stories, and stories travel. The *lack* of decencies also creates stories, stories that are often long-lasting.

Decencies define the signals that organizations send to their internal and external audiences. The unifying theme of these messages rounds out a set of norms that clearly define the limits between acceptable and unacceptable behavior. The messages help the participants act genuinely as members of a community. The messages are so ingrained that they give the members of the community confidence to assert, "That's not how we do things around here" when faced with a violation of the culture.

The Two-Minute Schmooze

Our exposure to the power of decencies started with the two-minute schmooze.

Steve Harrison is one of three founders of Lee Hecht Harrison, the world's leading career management company. At one point, the time was right to bring on a chief operating officer. The company needed an executive to handle the day-to-day responsibilities of running a rapidly growing company with offices in more than 25 cities across the United States. The COO the company hired was named Ray. He had an MBA and had recently retired from the US Army with the rank of brigadier general.

Steve decided to take Ray on a tour of the company so he could get to know as many people as possible.

Steve and Ray started their tour with several branch offices in the Northeast. At midmorning, the team arrived at their first stop, a midsized branch, and passed through the glass doors into the familiar reception area. Melissa, the receptionist, was on duty.

"How are you, Melissa?" Steve asked casually as they approached the reception desk.

"Fine. And you, Steve?"

"Great. Have a good day."

"You too."

Steve then proceeded toward the interior offices. Suddenly, he found himself being pulled back into the reception area. Ray looked agitated.

"What's wrong?" Steve asked Ray.

Ray said nothing. Instead, he firmly guided Steve back to the reception desk. Then Steve watched as Ray made an ally and a memory. The first thing Ray did was shake hands, show his charismatic smile, and say, "Good morning, Melissa, I'm Ray. I'll be the new COO. It's so great to meet you!"

After introducing himself, Ray launched into a dialogue with Melissa. "How long have you been with us?" "How did you hear about us?" "What did you do before you joined our firm?" "What kind of dog is that in the picture?" "What do you think of this business we're in together?" The collaborative language was infectious. It communicated that Ray and Melissa were together in an enterprise as equal partners.

Nor did the questioning go just one way.

Ray asked Melissa if she had any questions. He waited. Eventually, Melissa did ask a couple of questions, and Ray answered them candidly. Melissa was clearly delighted with the exchange.

Finally, Ray said, "Well, really nice to meet you, Melissa. Keep doin' what you're doin'. We need you! I look forward to seeing you next time I'm here." And with that Ray and Steve went inside to meet the rest of the staff.

As the team exited the reception area, Steve asked Ray, "What was that all about?"

"Steve," Ray said, "that's called the two-minute schmooze! Receptionists meet or talk by phone to more people critical to our company in one month than you or I could ever meet during a year: people at all levels, from all our branches everywhere, our customers, our suppliers, our colleagues, our bosses, our applicants, and job seekers. Most of all receptionists talk to each other. Melissa and the dozens like her at the firm serve as nothing less than our concierge desk. They are a key part of our reputation. And anyway, it's just the decent thing to do."

The decent thing to do. Of course, Steve had heard those words before, but hadn't put them in a work context in such a focused way. Ray's two-minute schmooze is how Steve first learned of the power of small decencies, and it's a perfect illustration of decent leadership and the impact it can have on organizations.

Decency Signals

Decency messages signal many things. "Warm and fuzzy" may be one of them, and that's okay. But there's an element of rigor to decencies, especially if we want them to be effective on a large scale. Based on our experience, effective decencies have many of the following characteristics:

Actionable. Organizations change by changing behavior. A decency is both an action and a catalyst for action. A decent act signals an immediate change in the behavior of the manager who offers it. The behavior of the person who receives the decency may also change. He or she may be inspired by the decency to perform better or communicate more effectively, or he or she may emulate the decency to other coworkers. Taken together, the initial action and the catalyzed action enhance the culture of the organization. Ray's two-minute schmooze was a discreet action—a conversation—that was a catalyst to encourage other managers to perform the same behavior.

Tangible. A decency can produce a measurable change to the environment. An intangible decency, by contrast, is a virtue, such as integrity or honesty. These are desirable qualities to strive for. But when these qualities are expressed in a way that is tangible, vivid, and, most of all, replicable, then virtues become decencies. They are perceptible by the senses and memorable. Melissa, the receptionist, probably recalled and recounted the specifics of her conversation with Ray many years later.

Affordable. A business decency must be within the financial means of the manager or organization. Small decencies, by definition, incur little or no investment. Ray's two-minute schmooze was free to the company. Small decencies must also be affordable in other ways. They shouldn't encumber the organization with undue overhead, unfunded mandates, legal liability, or counterproductive precedents.

Replicable. Decencies need to be replicable and scalable. Repeating the two-minute schmooze just strengthens its power. A decency offered to an individual is always welcome, but if the gesture is so constituted that it can be offered to only one individual, it may not rise to the level of a small decency. It's a one-off. A small decency works like ripples in a pond, creating impact and repetition far from the origin.

Sustainable. Decencies are best when they are implemented for today but are also available for the future. A decency is sustainable when the goodwill it generates for the organization over the long run more than compensates for the resources invested in it. We like to think that the two-minute schmooze became more widespread in the organization.

Starbucks Decencies

We end this discussion with an example of how a corporation makes decency actionable. Starbucks' CEO Howard Schultz has been a persistent champion of decency at work. In their 2014 annual meeting, he talked with investors about the role of corporations to "use our scale for good."

Every business today must confront often unfamiliar issues. Three examples are diversity, inclusion, and equity. These are more than fashionable buzzwords. They are business and often legal imperatives. Companies with inclusive practices in hiring, promotion, development, leadership, and team management generate up to 30 percent higher revenue per employee and greater profitability than their competitors, according to research from Deloitte.[1] Authentic inclusion values each employee and the wealth of experiences they bring to the job, thus inspiring and empowering people to want to give more to the organization.

Leaders can be proactive, or they can be reactive. In either case, leaders will find themselves forced to have an important conversation. Recall, for example, what happened when Starbucks faced an uproar following the arrest of two black men after a store manager called police. After a half-hearted attempt to support the store manager, CEO Howard Schultz acknowledged that the store manager had made a mistake and unconscious bias was the issue. In response, in a closely watched decision, Starbucks closed more than 8,000 of its company-owned stores for several hours on May 29, 2018, to provide racial bias training for 175,000 workers. The move signaled how important the company considered the incident and how committed it was to provide the training so a similar incident would not reoccur.

Instead of "let's find the racists among us and fix them or remove them," the company recognized that unconscious bias is a structural problem. Pointing fingers and placing blame is never the answer. Implicit bias training starts by helping workers understand that many biases are ingrained. That insight is generally reinforced by role-playing exercises designed to reveal how biases play out in the workplace and operationalized by offering strategies for tackling those ingrained biases at work.

To underscore his commitment to decencies at work, Schultz published a two-page advertisement in the *New York Times* and the *Wall Street Journal*. The ads, in stark black and white, listed the foundational basis for any culture of decencies. As of this writing, the 48-year tradition of quality food products and innovative culture continue throughout Starbucks' 30,000 locations globally.

CHAPTER 4

THE BUSINESS CASE FOR DECENCY

> *"PhD in Leadership. Short course:*
> *Make a short list of all things done to you that you abhorred.*
> *Don't do them to others. Ever.*
> *Make another list of things done to you that you loved.*
> *Do them to others. Always."*
>
> **—TOM PETERS**

Leaders acknowledge that, by every measure, human assets represent the critical difference between corporate success and failure. Now more than ever, responsible leaders understand the connection between decency and employee retention and engagement. The best leaders know that a deterioration of civility leads to the decline of employment retention and engagement.

Developing and nurturing talent is a significant driver of employee engagement, which in turn is the key to the outcomes all businesses seek: revenue, profitability, quality, innovation, reputation, and customer loyalty. Talent shortage is not just a demographic issue. It is, leaders would agree, a matter of how well a pattern of decency is embedded in the corporate culture.

Every business assures us that its greatest asset is its employees. It's pretty callous to refer to human beings as assets in any case. This assurance is often little more than lip service. One would hope businesses would do everything in their power to treat their employees well. In fact, as we see every day, a great deal of daylight can exist between what businesses say they value and what, by their behavior, they actually value.

CNN Money reported that 84 percent of America's workers were unhappy with their current positions.[1] Mercer's "What's Working" survey found that one in three US employees are serious about leaving their current jobs.[2]

Gratitude, focusing on positive experiences, exercising, and random acts of kindness are all ways to change the pattern through which our brain views work. This conclusion is the thrust of "The Price of Incivility: Lack of Respect Hurts Morale and the Bottom Line," published in the *Harvard Business Review*.[3] The research, polling managers and employees in 17 industries, revealed the high price organizations pay for workers who have been on the receiving end of indecency at work. Specifically, the research concluded that:

- 80% lost work time worrying about the incident.
- 78% said their commitment to the organization declined.

- 66% said their performance declined.
- 63% lost work time avoiding the offender.
- 48% intentionally decreased their work effort.
- 47% intentionally decreased the time spent at work.
- 38% intentionally decreased the quality of their work.
- 25% admitted taking their frustration out on customers.
- 12% said that they left their jobs because of the uncivil treatment.

The Cost of Turnover

Employee retention is one benefit of high employee engagement. Experience shows that when engagement goes down, employee turnover goes up. It's also well understood that employee turnover is expensive, but less well understood is how expensive. A recent report by *Forbes* magazine estimates that employee turnover alone cost US companies $160 billion in 2017 in recruitment, administration, lost productivity, and retraining.[4]

Some turnover is necessary for healthy organizations. For employees, turnover can represent opportunity. Improving economic conditions make it easier for employees to switch jobs and pursue their career goals. It is well known in organizational development that employees generally don't quit their companies, they quit their supervisors. According to the *Washington Post*, when employees quit, of the seven most common reasons given for quitting, six have to do with the behavior of their direct managers:

- Isolated or disconnected manager
- Lack of feeling supported by their manager
- Disrespect from their manager
- Confusing priorities and expectations from management
- Low or no growth opportunities
- Inadequate coaching
- Lack of feedback from their manager[5]

Decent Benefits

Leaders are often uncertain about what their employees want. Or, worse, they make assumptions. Invariably, the default hypothesis is that what employees want most are material benefits: more money, more vacation, better parking, better food in the cafeteria, more perks. The assumption continues that the more material benefits employees have, the happier they will be and the less they will want to quit.

Haven't companies learned that the basis of customer satisfaction is listening to their customers? Why would they forget that lesson when it comes to engaging with their employees? So, the first step is to get leaders to ask their employees: What would inspire you to be more committed? More engaged? More aligned with the mission?

Research shows that there is a big disconnect between what leaders think employees want and what employees say they want.[6] Had leaders asked fewer questions (most of these engagement studies involve asking employees more than a hundred questions), then listened to and taken action on the answers the questions produced, leaders would have learned that while material benefits are important, there are other issues that are far more important. The worst part is, when employees are asked the same questions repeatedly yet all their answers are still ignored, they learn to have little expectation that any meaningful change will occur. Consider this side-by-side comparison:

Assumption *What leaders think employees want*	Reality *What employees really want*
Money as an end in itself	Money as evidence of being valued
Retirement plan for the future	A today plan with a sense of purpose
Workplace perks	Control, flexible hours, remote work
Company-paid benefits (e.g., car, phone, health club membership)	A sense of pride and mission; leaders who listen
To be managed well	To be coached well
Annual performance review	Ongoing performance review
Promotion opportunities	Development opportunities, even if that development isn't necessarily upward
Clear rules	To be treated fairly
Clear expectations	Knowing they are heard, a belief that the work they are doing is important to the organization

Let's be clear. Inadequate material benefits, such as a salary not commensurate with experience or fewer benefits than prevailing industry norms, will certainly lead to increased turnover. It's the reciprocal assumption—that more material benefits over a certain point will lead to more engagement—that is not supported by research.

The reality is that what employees are truly looking for goes beyond material benefits or perks that can be counted on a spreadsheet. Rather, employees are looking for work that provides a sense of meaning and personal satisfaction in working conditions that can be described by the word "decent."

Most relevant research supports this view. "Many researchers who have studied retention agree on what engages or satisfies people and therefore influences them to stay: meaningful and challenging work, a chance to learn and grow, fair and competitive compensation, great coworkers, recognition, respect, and a good boss," write Beverly Kaye and Sharon Jordan-Evans in their book *Love 'Em or Lose 'Em: Getting Good People to Stay*. It's no longer enough to simply throw "material" things at employees and expect them to remain engaged.

Employee Needs Are in Flux

It's also important to note that what motivates employees today may change tomorrow. The needs of employees are always in flux. This fact challenges managers to find new ways to motivate, inspire, and reward their people. Otherwise, employees will keep jumping from job to job in a quest to satisfy the need they have for meaning at work. A culture of decencies works to get ahead of the turnover curve. Such a culture encourages companies to demonstrate to both potential and active employees that they can realistically expect to find:

A connection to—even passion in—their work. Employee engagement and retention are closely linked; workers who feel passionate about their jobs are less likely to leave.

"Passion for work means that people find what they do to be so exciting that it sometimes doesn't even feel like work—so exciting that it brings exhilaration, a 'high,'" write Beverly Kaye and Sharon Jordan-Evans. "Granted, even those who have this passion seldom have it every day, but they do know that feeling, and they know when they lose it."

Respect for their contributions. Many managers feel that if they don't exhibit some sort of command-control, they won't get the most from their employees. However, as evidenced by the growing practice of servant leadership, hierarchical models are becoming increasingly outdated and rejected by a millennial workforce. Providing employees with a "seat at the table" and an opportunity to share their opinions without fear is a critical way to show respect, driving the alignment between what managers want and what employees need. Showing trust, understanding, and fairness inspires employees to reflect those qualities back, ultimately improving productivity and creating a more dedicated workforce.

A Form of "Goodwill Banking"

All of this demonstrates that the role of decency is more than a desirable artifact of an organizational culture when business conditions make it affordable. It is not a compromise to productivity or quality. It does not impede competitiveness. Decency is a form of "goodwill banking," an accelerant to innovation and value-driven excellence. Finally, decencies can help inoculate the corporate culture against the kinds of opportunism and expediency that invite ethical lapses and corporate crises.

How do decencies work? Let's consider the hiring process. For the job seeker, what are the indicators of corporate decency? The reception area often determines the prospective employee's first impression of the company. How is the visitor welcomed? As a valued source of expertise for the organization or as another bother? Is the receptionist friendly or distracted? Is there a physical barrier between the visitor and the receptionist? Does he or she multitask to a fault?

"Look for the telltale signs," author John Cowan writes. Character always reveals itself. He goes on to suggest that "we can be true to our values both at home and at work . . . the more humanely we treat one another, the better we will be as people, and the better we will be at doing our life's work." Decencies, to be culturally impactful, need to be actionable, tangible, practical, affordable, replicable, and sustainable. Decencies are a cultural gift. They create stories—and stories travel, even faster than photocopied values statements.

There are other signs of cultural decency, too. How prepared are the hiring authorities? Are they focused? Do they take steps to demonstrate the importance of the interview by, say, turning off their phones or otherwise seeing to it that the meeting is uninterrupted? Do they demonstrate a willingness to not just take, but to give, information? Is the visitor provided the opportunity to ask questions, and if so, are those questions answered specifically? Is there a prompt and smooth handoff to a second interviewer, if there is one? At the end, is there clear commitment to next steps, and if so, are the commitments honored? Is the visitor courteously escorted back to the reception area?

Finally, enlightened leaders understand the benefits of treating unsuccessful applicants decently. Quite apart from treating people with dignity and respect, it must be remembered that rejected applicants add another voice to the conversations that determine a company's reputation and brand. One leader who understood this truth was Herb Kohl, the son of the founder of Kohl's, with 1,158 locations, currently one of the largest department store chains in the United States. Founded in 1927 by Polish immigrant Maxwell Kohl, the chain developed a reputation of treating employees well. "Every employee is going to have a last day," says Ryan Festerling, former vice president of human resources at Kohl's. "You can't ask people to be brand ambassadors if you don't treat them well on the way out."

A recent "Preoccupations" feature article in the *New York Times* was titled, "Be Nice to Job Seekers (They're Shoppers, Too)."[7] When the way an organization interacts with job candidates is devoid of basic professional courtesies, selection quality suffers, retention goes down, and hiring costs go up. The interactions decency engenders are not costly: prompt responses to phone calls and e-mails, personalized attention, and frequent "keep in the loop" communications.

In our new world, candidates' correspondence to companies is rarely acknowledged. Calls are seldom returned. Status updates are not routinely provided. Rejection decisions are not consistently communicated. All this combines to create the job-search black hole. A business can lose sight that there are real people behind all those résumés, and how the company treats those people says a lot about it, its brand, and its values.

This may sound like recruitment best practices, but the reality is that many employers become so transactional in their hiring that some of these decencies are forgotten. The unfortunate reality of hiring is that there will always be more people rejected than hired. To the extent companies can moderate the blow of rejection, they may reap unexpected benefits.

A Stanford University case study revealed that a few employers get this concept.[8] These companies recognize that employment candidates are also or might become customers. At Nabisco, for example, a manager declared that his company responds to every résumé. When asked why, he said, "Because everyone eats cookies."

Human Touch Matters

Consultants and business journals are not alone in highlighting the essential mandate of the human factor. Robert

Reich, in his book *The Future of Success*, writes: "Human touch matters: in restaurants, banks, medical care, hotels and spas. Personal attention is not a frill, it's a necessity." Reich, the former US Secretary of Labor, sums it up in two words: "Compassionate Capitalism."

When Herb Baum, ex-CEO of Dial Corporation, routinely sat down with small employee groups for "Hot Dogs with Herb," he understood the power of decency. When the leadership at W. L. Gore (Gore-Tex) created and sustained a failure-tolerant innovation culture, they understood the power of decency. When Doug Conant, ex-CEO of the Campbell Soup Company, routinely handwrote thank-you notes to deserving employees around the world, he understood the power of decency. And when the late poet Maya Angelou said, "I've learned in my life that people will forget what you said, they'll even forget what you did, but they'll never forget how you made them feel," she recognized the power of decency.

Employee Engagement at Microsoft

When Satya Nadella took over the job of CEO from legendary Microsoft founder Bill Gates and his successor Steve Ballmer, he had big shoes to fill. Nadella wanted to shift the company's culture. Specifically, he was determined to disrupt a corporate culture long recognized as a nest of intense infighting and silos competing with other silos. That would start by recognizing what employees did well rather than what they did wrong.

After becoming CEO in 2014, Nadella asked all top executives at Microsoft to commit to empathic collaboration. The gesture signaled that Nadella planned to run the company differently from his well-known predecessors. The first step was to address Microsoft's practice of infighting. He took a number of steps. The first was to encourage humility. He did this by modeling vulnerability. When he did not know something, Nadella said so. He wasn't afraid to ask for help. He challenged the company's 125,000 employees around the world to reject a culture of arrogance ("we know it all") and embrace a culture of curiosity ("we learn it all"). That change has led all stakeholders—customers, partners, and investors—to engage with the company in new, more collaborative ways.

As a result of reorienting the culture, the tenor of almost every Microsoft interaction began to change. Meetings grew more relaxed and productive. Under the previous CEOs, collaboration at Microsoft often saw employees showing off how much they knew (or pretended to know) and jostling for credit and resources. Every participant spent inordinate amounts of time preparing for meetings by appearing to have all the answers and having solutions that were bulletproof to the criticisms of the CEO. The downside of that approach was that it left little room for uncertainty, searching, or collaboration.

Nadella's approach favors humility. The meetings he runs are organized around the assumptions that humility and vulnerability are essential not only for inspiring cooperation in the office but also for creating products and services that resonate with real customers. As part of this goal, Nadella updated Microsoft's mission statement from something transactional:

A PC on every desk and in every home, running Microsoft software.

to something transformational:

To empower every person and every organization on the planet to achieve more.

Which vision statement is more engaging?

Nadella insists that vulnerability is a strength at Microsoft. He wants the culture to focus on growth and skills the organization has yet to master versus preserving market share using skills it has already mastered. The reward is that corporate cultures focused on growth make it their mission to learn new things, understanding that they won't succeed at all of them.

Yes, this approach increases risk and the real possibility of failure. Failure is the price an organization occasionally pays for real innovation. Nadella wrote off Microsoft's $7 billion acquisition of Nokia's mobile phone business as a total loss, acknowledging that Windows lost the battle to be a player in the operating system for mobile phones. It's not clear that Ballmer, who made the decision to acquire Nokia, would have been so likely to accept such a high-profile failure.

Purpose Statements Build Authenticity

Enterprises are turning to "purpose" and "authenticity" as a way to engage employees and customers alike. It is critical that enterprises brand themselves with a clearly articulated vision and authentic social purpose. This is where a succinct purpose statement comes in. We believe every company can profit by formulating such a vision or purpose statement. The statement can be grand and aspirational. Most importantly, the company, by its daily actions, should be seen by stakeholders as living up to the statement.

Consider a few of our favorite purpose statements:

Starbucks: To inspire and nurture the human spirit—one person, one cup of coffee at a time.

3M: To advance every life and improve every business while using science to solve the world's greatest challenges.

Pepsi-Cola: To improve all aspects of the world in which we operate—environmental, social, economic—creating a better tomorrow than today.

Adidas: To be the global leader in the sporting goods industry with brands built on a passion for sports and a sporting lifestyle.

Nike: To bring inspiration and innovation to every athlete in the world.

Let's compare the Nike and Adidas purpose statements. We appreciate the Nike vision statement because, while it seems unnecessarily restrictive ("every athlete"), it soon becomes clear that Nike believes that by virtue of having a body every human being in the world is an athlete. Which statement resonates more? Which one better speaks to you, regardless of whether you are a customer, partner, or investor? We give the edge to Nike. Besides being wordier, Adidas puts the emphasis on a sporting lifestyle. That's fair. But using half as many words, the Nike statement addresses not only people's interests but their sense of who they are.

The vision statement needs to be cocreated by consultation with all stakeholders. Employees are not just workers. Employees are cocreators. They want the purpose to be their own. Purpose needs to be shared.

PricewaterhouseCooper's Bottom-Up Mission Statement

The accounting and auditing firm PricewaterhouseCooper (doing business as PwC) recently completed a bottom-up, multiyear project to define its mission statement and values. By bottom-up, we mean the project saw more than 200,000 PwC employees in dozens of countries participating in the program. Unlike most corporate branding initiatives, which are conceived at the top, PwC let employees generate the content and wording of their mission statement. Here is the powerful product of this approach:

Our purpose is to build trust in society and solve important problems.

Note that for the company's purpose, the employees emphasized not the actual services the company offers—accounting and auditing—but something far more encompassing: trust in the service of solving important problems. We are impressed by the results of this exercise and commend the bottom-up approach to other organizations. PwC's mission statement goes on to say:

> *Our purpose is why we exist. Our values define how we behave. In an increasingly complex world, we help intricate systems function, adapt and evolve so they can benefit communities and society—whether they are capital markets, tax systems or the economic systems within which business and society exist. We help our clients to make informed decisions and operate effectively within them.*

After this general statement, the PwC code identifies the set of values and behaviors that PwC stakeholders are required to honor if they wish to remain associated with the global PwC community. The guide holds everyone, including leaders, to account for doing their best.

Specifically, when "working with our clients and our colleagues to build trust in society and solve important problems, we . . .

- Speak up for what is right, especially when it feels difficult
- Expect and deliver the highest quality outcomes

- Make decisions and act as if our personal reputations were at stake
- Stay informed and ask questions about the future of the world we live in
- Create impact with our colleagues, our clients and society through our actions
- Respond with agility to the ever-changing environment in which we operate
- Make the effort to understand every individual and what matters to them
- Recognize the value that each person contributes
- Support others to grow and work in the ways that bring out their best
- Collaborate and share relationships, ideas and knowledge beyond boundaries
- Seek and integrate a diverse range of perspectives, people and ideas
- Give and ask for feedback to improve ourselves and others
- Dare to challenge the status quo and try new things
- Innovate, test and learn from failure
- Have an open mind to the possibilities in every idea

Your Purpose Statement

We encourage every company to articulate a shared purpose statement. The task is difficult, especially if you do it the right way by involving thousands of stakeholders at every level of the organization and building the statement from the bottom up. Logistics aside, the task starts by every stakeholder engaging with questions that start with the words "What is the shared purpose?"

- What is the shared purpose that we and our customers can work on together?
- What is the shared purpose that is a natural expression of who we are and what we stand for?
- What is the shared purpose that connects how we make money and how we contribute to the world?

Decencies are baked into the shared purpose statement by creating an organizational culture that ensures that the firm's purpose and values are always the screen through which decisions big and small are made. When things are going well and profits are good, there is usually little risk to the congruence between purpose and behavior. But every enterprise faces tough economic times. These are the moments of truth when the purpose statement is tested and the company answers for itself the question of how much it actually values its culture and principles.

A good test of whether a company is acting in congruence with its purpose statement is to consider whether a proposed course of action is at the core of the decision. All the examples of corporate malfeasance that we have considered in this book readily fail this test. It will be remembered that Wells Fargo CEO John Stumpf, for example, lost his job when it was revealed that bank employees routinely opened new accounts and issued insurance policies and credit cards for customers who had not requested them.

In doing so, the company demonstrated that their purpose was not at center stage of their actions. When purpose is at the center of the action, the results are a lot different. Whole Foods, for example, won applause by selling only seafood that was certified as sustainable. Even though the higher prices of certified seafood translated into decreased sales, Whole Foods maintained the principle.

If the "little things" (small but meaningful gestures) take hold and become pervasive, they create stories and patterns and textures that can enrich a culture. These little things have power because they can be felt every day by everyone. They become a unifying experience that becomes sustainable by the force of everyone repeating them.

An "ethical culture" should be seen as part of the tangible, homegrown, specific behaviors and time-honored traditions that form the fabric of an organization, help ensure its sustainability, and help reduce its vulnerability. It's as if to say, "That's how we do things around here."

CHAPTER 5

THE ELEMENTS OF DECENCY AND HOW THEY WORK TOGETHER

> *"The only thing of real importance that leaders do is to create and manage culture."*
>
> **—EDGAR SCHEIN**

Common decency is not necessarily the term most associated with the business world today. If news headlines are a guide, a case can be made that decency is one of the less frequently used tools that leaders have in their management toolbox.

News reports and headlines tend to focus on the negative. Indecency creates conflict, and conflict attracts viewers. There is no news value perceived in headlines such as "Business Leader Handles Difficult Situation with

Decency." But when a CEO is caught cheating, overstepping his or her authority, or acting indecently, the headlines are all over it. It's appropriate for CEOs and other business leaders to be held accountable when they make mistakes. It's also appropriate for CEOs to be recognized when they act with integrity. Accountability flows both ways.

Leadership is about motivating people to do what must be done, achieving results through the coordinated efforts of others. Our experience demonstrates that despite all the negative news, business leaders around the world have concluded that a culture of decencies creates favorable conditions and outcomes. The outcomes are easily measured. Colleagues, employees, and partners who are treated decently and respectfully are much more engaged in the mission of the enterprise than those who are not.

Higher levels of employee engagement have been associated with bottom-line outcomes, such as lower turnover, increased innovation, fewer failures, a more resilient culture, and superior financial performance. A practice of small decencies can be defended on the basis that it is the "right thing to do," and it can be justified by the bottom-line impact it has on the outcomes most important to any organization.

Small Decencies

Small decencies are individual gestures that help define the larger environment and thereby become the building blocks of an ethical culture. Regulatory approaches to making corporations more law-abiding and ethical were supposed to restore investor confidence through greater transparency, increased accountability, and improved governance. However, evidence shows that the unintended consequences are ham-fisted responses by companies reacting to heavy-handed regulations. Regulations or appeals to command and control by themselves can't move the needle to create well-behaved companies. Effective leadership supported by a culture of decencies can.

The impact of small decencies can be large. An example may help.

Before his current role as partner at Score Recruitment (great motto: "Where Aptitude Meets Attitude!"), Rick Klein was president of TMP Worldwide, a leader in national directory/search programs. While he was at TMP, Rick introduced one of the most inspiring decencies we're aware of. He called it "Fulghum Days," and every TMP worker received one as an extra day off. Rick's only request: employees could do whatever they wanted with their Fulghum Day except anything related to work or TMP Worldwide.

Rick got the idea for Fulghum Days by reading Robert Fulghum's *All I Need to Know I Learned in Kindergarten*, a 1988 book that came to be enormously popular. The book begins with a list of practices—decencies, really—emphasized in kindergarten that the author suggested could serve people well in all walks of life. You probably recognize some of the lessons:

- Share everything
- Play fair
- Don't hit people
- Put things back where you found them
- Clean up your own mess
- Don't take things that aren't yours
- Say you're sorry when you hurt somebody
- Take a nap every afternoon
- When you go out into the world, watch out for traffic, hold hands, and stick together

Thanks to decencies like this, TMP's employees cherished their boss and worked harder than ever to be worthy of Fulghum Days. TMP clients recognized the enthusiasm of the employees and responded with more assignments. Revenues increased and turnover decreased. One employee was so touched by Rick's gesture that he wrote a letter to the author requesting that Fulghum sign a copy of the book and send it to Rick. The author not only signed a book, he wrote Rick a personal note expressing his appreciation for so well understanding the real meaning of the book. Rick framed the letter along with the inscription on the book and displayed it for years in his office. It may still be there.

The Bubble Wrap

Small decencies are the "bubble wrap" that keeps a corporate culture intact. They fertilize the playing field for innovation. They may represent only 2 percent of what we do, but 98 percent of who we are. They satisfy the ultimate test of cultural health: How does it feel to live in this environment and be shaped by it? "Organizations have a feel about them," says Charles Handy in *The Hungry Spirit*, ". . . a feel which the visitor picks up as soon as he or she enters the building or, often, merely encounters one of the people who work there." Small decencies release that feel.

In the current labor market, some companies think they can afford to skimp on what they mistakenly refer to as "niceties." They are mistaken, though, because every economic cycle eventually turns, and there is always competition for the best talent. Company leaders need to treat job candidates like customers. A Stanford University case study found that some companies get this concept.[1] They recognize that employment candidates also have a dual role as customers.

Telltale Signs

Look for the telltale signs of small decencies. We talk of decent acts, a decent wage, a decent fellow, or "are you decent?" The thesaurus is helpful: "Considerate, courteous, gracious, honest, honorable, thoughtful, appropriate, tasteful, respectable, helpful, civil." In the corporate setting, decency has a vital place in giving shape and sustainability to a culture.

As seemingly trite and sentimental as these examples are, they are an apt prelude to vivid examples in corporate life. When one corporate executive made sure his receptionists displayed their own business cards with the title "Director of First Impressions," he understood the power of decency. When the founder and chairman of the Wegmans food chain created the "Hardship Fund" for employees in unexpected need, he understood the power of decency.

The role of decency has little to do with softness or indecisiveness. Rather, it's a form of "goodwill banking," an accumulation of institutionalized gestures that help pave the way for a business to make it through the inevitable tough times.

"Sometimes it's the smallest acts that influence other people months or even years later," suggests Joseph L. Badaracco Jr., author of *Leading Quietly*. These are the behaviors that in a post-compliance world will lead to good citizenship, stewardship, profit, and success. By fertilizing the ground of corporate cultures with decencies, legal compliance initiatives can more easily take root. The decencies described in this book can help ready an organization to adhere to regulatory requirements in a hopeful context. They can serve as a tonic that may relieve the counterproductive effects of our commercial dynamism. When combined with the necessary laws, regulations, and governance, the result can be organizations we can be proud of.

Choose Another Path

Sometimes decency is best represented by what CEOs and other leaders reject doing. In this regard, Jim Lukaszewski's

Civility and Decency Manifesto is celebrated as a concise, specific series of actions that will avoid crossing the line to incivility and indecency:

- When your words, deeds, or actions turn to vilification, stop.
- When you use sarcasm to ridicule and damage, demean, dismiss, diminish, or humiliate, stop.
- When your words are arrogant, causing needless but intentional pain and suffering, stop.
- When your words clearly express anger and irritation, stop.
- When your words, deeds, or actions are demanding and bullying, stop.
- When your words are just plain mean, stop.
- When your words insult, stop.
- When your words become corrosive and disrespectful, stop.
- When your words become disparaging and tone deaf, stop.
- When you speak and behave without empathy, stop, reconsider.
- When your words mindlessly injure, stop.
- When your words, deeds, or actions intentionally injure, stop.
- When your words spread accusations and suspicion, stop.
- When your words exhibit overbearance and overzealousness, stop.

- When what you propose is negative, punitive, defensive, and harmfully restrictive on others, stop. Choose another pathway.
- When your words exceed the boundaries of decency, civility, and integrity, just simply stop. Choose another path.

The true test of decency is a commitment to verbal and written communication that is predominantly positive and declarative and behaviors that are simple, sensible, constructive, positive, empathetic, and beneficial to the recipient out of proportion to the sender. Any other pathways lead only to trouble, prolong problems, and delay mitigation and resolution. Empathy means positive deeds that speak louder and more constructively than words.

Decencies "Wall of Fame"

- *Value receptionists: They are your "Directors of First Impressions."*
- *Downsize with dignity: You're making memories.*
- *Model trust: Accessibility, transparency, candor.*
- *Recognition: Thank you psychic income.*
- *Praise in public; criticize in private.*[2]
- *Reject executive pomposity.*
- *Forget "open-door" policy: It's about MBWA.*
- *Avoid symbols of hypocrisy and mixed messages.*
- *Tolerate innovation failure; celebrate success.*
- *Recognize people in unglamorous jobs.*
- *Institutionalize civility.*
- *Call out harassment and bullying.*
- *Share credit; hoard blame.*
- *Remember names.*
- *Embrace diversity.*
- *Don't multitask in meetings.*
- *For meetings you schedule, be the first to arrive and the last to leave.*
- *In multinational settings, avoid slang, idioms, colloquialisms.*
- *Be first in line for compliance training.*
- *DWYSYWD: Do what you say you will do!*

CHAPTER 6

DECENCIES ARE CONTAGIOUS

> *"How people are treated increasingly determines whether a company will prosper and even survive."*
> **—ED LAWLER**

ospitals around the country have learned the value of decency especially well because they have measured the costs imposed by doctors and staff who are indifferent to decency. Indifference to decency leads to bad outcomes: breakdowns in process, more medical errors, more lawsuits, resentful patients, resentful juries, and costlier judgments.

Every hospital has its share of what the medical industry calls "temperamental doctors." Read this as rude and arrogant doctors. These doctors may be technically skilled but have somehow missed the bulletin about the importance of humility and empathy. When lawsuits occur, these doctors often tend to be involved.

In response to the issue of temperamental doctors, hospitals around the country are requiring doctors who have incivility complaints lodged against them to attend what the administrators call "charm school." This training in empathy is intended to minimize unnecessary impatience, arrogance, harshness, and other behaviors that lead to everything from negative patient reviews to complaints to lawsuits. What these trainings really focus on, when all is said and done, are *decencies*.

Los Angeles hospitals have taken the lead in insisting that doctors set the tone for their medical residents. This is an example of "tone at the top" at its most critical, as human lives are at stake. Hospitals subscribing to this effort train their workers to look out for unreported instances of incivility, such as impatiently cutting corners, ignoring handwashing protocols, and nurses refusing to work with doctors.

At Johns Hopkins Bayview Medical Center in Baltimore, decency is a core tenet of what is expected of every physician and support staff. Every employee receives a laminated card with 10 tips on maintaining civil discourse and behavior at work. The Center reports that decency in its workplace builds stronger, more productive teams that deliver the highest-quality healthcare to patients.[1]

Normally, the absence of decencies isn't a matter of literal life and death, so the hospital example is a special case. But a culture of indecency among physicians in their workplace can rob support staff of motivation and empathy. Every organization is better off when the leaders set a tone of coaching their followers for decency. This coaching takes several forms. It depends less on what the leaders say they value and more on how they behave. Employees rightly look at what their leaders do—especially when the leaders think no one is looking—to evaluate whether they are worthy of that role.

Tone at the Top Matters

Many organizations have adopted rules for decency. The Irvine, California–based law firm Bryan Cave went through a visioning process where associates defined the behavior norms they valued for the practice and agreed on the rules for which they were willing to hold one another accountable. Ten norms were the basis of the firm's code of conduct. Shortly afterward, Bryan Cave was ranked number one on the list of the Best Places to Work in Orange County. Here is the firm's Code of Civility:

- We greet and acknowledge each other.
- We say please and thank you.
- We treat each other equally and with respect, no matter the conditions.
- We acknowledge the impact of our behavior on others.
- We welcome feedback from each other.
- We are approachable.
- We are direct, sensitive, and honest.
- We acknowledge the contributions of others.

- We respect each other's time commitments.
- We address incivility.

Zappos, the online shoe retailer, bakes an ethos of decency into its 10 core values. Each one of these values is founded on a sense that decency at every level of the organization is required to develop the value ownership that makes execution at a high level sustainable. The Ten Core Values of Zappos are:

- Deliver WOW Through Service
- Embrace and Drive Change
- Create Fun and a Little Weirdness
- Be Adventurous, Creative, and Open-Minded
- Pursue Growth and Learning
- Build Open and Honest Relationships with Communication
- Build a Positive Team and Family Spirit
- Do More with Less
- Be Passionate and Determined
- Be Humble

Bottom-Line Value

Organizations can reap significant bottom-line value when committing to a culture of decency. When organizations adopted ethics and compliance principles, even to a minimum standard, employees were 132 percent more likely to report misconduct and 270 percent more likely to be satisfied with the organization's response compared with an organization with no program, according to the 2018 Global Business Ethics Survey, a report by the Ethics and Compliance Initiative.[2] The Ethics and Compliance Initiative (ECI) is the oldest ethics research and best practice community in the United States. The findings of the report focus on the impact that an ethics and compliance (E&C) program has in the workplace and the return on investment (ROI) for program development and improvement.

The findings of the report, "Measuring the Impact of E&C Programs," are significant. Since its release, hundreds of E&C practitioners have been trained using these principles. The report demonstrates that as the quality and strength of ethics and compliance programs increase, organizations see improvements in several key performance areas, including the establishment of a stronger, more resilient culture and significant decrease in misconduct. ECI also found that adhering to any of the 15 operational standards of a high-quality ethics and compliance framework resulted in a dramatic return on investment.

In organizations where ethics and compliance take a front seat, employees demonstrated a tenfold increase in confidence and trust in the organization. "This report makes the case that when it comes to ethics and compliance programs, every effort by an organization makes a difference," said Patricia Harned, CEO of ECI. "Yet program quality matters—the higher the quality, the higher the ROI for the organization."[3]

Cultural Guide Rails

Decencies serve as guide rails for protecting the company culture. When crafted with intention, delivered with resolve, and honored even when the going gets rough, decency encourages employees to make good decisions, to take the correct action, and to hold their colleagues accountable when they violate the norms.

Coaching is an integral part of transmitting a culture of decencies. Coaching for decency focuses on helping followers learn to listen, to give and receive feedback, to avoid judging and accept personal responsibility, to work across differences, and to deal with difficulties head-on. Coaching is more than just imparting information.

Decency reminds us that we can be true to our values both at home and at work, and that the more humanely we treat one another, the better we will be as people and the better we will be in doing our life's work. The common thread is that ethical behavior is an expected side effect of focusing on something besides generating results. Let's focus, instead, on small business decencies for their own sake precisely because doing so brings meaning to the workplace. If we do that, we believe that the corporate cultures in which we operate will grow in the ways we desire.

All this is by way of saying that although we are businesspeople, we're people first. We are colleagues who can make a difference in another person's day, and we're people who want to be treated with respect, humanity, and care. Out of such actions, multiplied dozens of times a day, corporate cultures take root and sprout what George H. W. Bush called "a thousand points of light."

Decencies Inspire

When you think about the indelible stories defining an organization, decencies are invariably at their core. Decencies manufacture mobile memories; they form the foundation for traditions; and healthy traditions are the building blocks of great places to work. Indra Nooyi, for example, was the chairman of PepsiCo from 2007 to 2018. Her employee satisfaction ratings stood at 75 percent. Early in her role as CEO, it occurred to Nooyi that she had never thanked the parents of her hardworking executives for the gift of their child to PepsiCo. She started to write personal letters to the parents expressing her appreciation. It was always a positive report card. She wouldn't write anything less than complimentary.

The letters opened a floodgate of emotions. The parents were so delighted about receiving the letters, they told neighbors and extended family members. Decencies produce momentum, and as we have seen, they also create powerful stories.

Jim Lukaszewski recalls his first management training process to become a first line supervisor at the Schmitt

Company in Minneapolis. Supervisors were trained by managing different departments for a month. At one point Jim was put in charge of the stereo and hi-fi components department. This department had five of the most successful salespeople of these products in America. His assignments were simple: write at least one or two complimentary notes to each salesperson and conduct a sales meeting at 7:30 a.m. every Tuesday morning focusing on a fresh idea the salespeople could use. He was 26 years old at the time.

During the month Jim was in the department, one of its top salespeople passed away. His boss asked Jim to go through the employee's desk to make sure there was nothing embarrassing there because the family wanted to come in and spend some time in the area where this man had worked for so many years so successfully. As Jim went through the desk, he found a collection of papers in the back of the bottom drawer. It wasn't immediately clear why these papers were stored in the back of a desk drawer. But as Jim went through the items, he noticed they were in chronological order going back some 32 years. Each item was a letter or note to the salesperson with a compliment, and there on the top of the pile was the congratulatory note Jim had just given to this employee earlier in the week. The man had apparently saved every positive response he had ever gotten. Jim always interpreted this as an indication of the power of a timely note and a compliment. The family recognized almost all of them because he talked about them at home every time he got one.

Effective leaders use decencies to build great workforces one gesture at a time. Reuben Mark, former chairman and CEO of Colgate-Palmolive, credits his success to a simple decision. "I have made it my business to be sure that nothing important or creative at Colgate-Palmolive is perceived as my idea," Mark said.

At biotech company Genentech, every member of the leadership team has at least one "open office hour" each month—taking a cue from academia, where professors are available to students during office hours.

Jim Donald, former CEO and president of Starbucks, insisted that "hour-long" meetings be completed in 45 minutes. As a time-management technique, this policy improves efficiency and saves untold hours. But the small decency embedded in this policy is what Donald suggested meeting participants do with the freed-up 15 minutes. "I want you to use your extra 15 minutes to call someone you usually do not contact every day," he said.

As commissioner of Major League Baseball from 1984 to 1989, Peter Ueberroth attended dozens of baseball games every year. Most people don't know that every major league baseball stadium has a special box reserved for the commissioner, which invariably has the best view, food, and drink. "I never sat in one of those boxes," Ueberroth says. "Not once." When Ueberroth attended baseball games, he sat among the fans. Sometimes fans recognized him, but mostly they didn't. "I was a better commissioner of baseball for having so many conversations with regular fans," he says.

Every Incivility Creates
Permanent Damage

Rudeness and verbal bullying undermine the effective-ness of organizations large and small. The impact of verbal and gestural rudeness undermines performance equally at the bottom of the organization (at the level of work that delivers services to customers) and at the top (in the boardroom). Those who are on the receiving end of rude-ness or who simply witness rudeness tend to normalize the incivility and thereafter see the world through "rude-color glasses," imposing significant costs on organizations.

Rudeness from authority figures is a huge problem because it signals to everyone lower in the chain of com-mand that workplace indecency is acceptable. A study from the University of North Carolina, published by the *Journal of Applied Psychology*, adds to a growing body of research showing the economic pain caused by workplace rudeness.[4] Research has demonstrated that worker dis-engagement flows predictably from personal experiences of workplace rudeness, resulting in loss of revenue, time delays, and turnover.

Half of all workers report that they experience rude exchanges in the workplace at least weekly. The study defines rudeness as low-intensity deviant behavior with ambiguous intent to harm. When rudeness is tolerated or unchallenged, it is easy for corporate cultures to normal-ize indecency. It's a mistake for leaders to tolerate rudeness because, left unchecked, it's as contagious as the flu.

Workplace rudeness has long-lasting impact far beyond the individuals directly implicated. The secondhand effects of rudeness are often more destructive than the original acts because they can extend to every employee in the organization.

The adage "Sticks and stones may break your bones, but words will never harm you" is simply a lie. Injuries from sticks and stones will heal. An insult, an embarrassing statement, a humiliating confrontation leaves no scars, no visible wounds, no bleeding, but everyone remembers an insult, an embarrassment, a mean-spirited comment by somebody that may have happened years ago. What we learn from working with the victims of verbal assault is that the damage caused is usually permanent.

When rudeness is normalized, every employee is on alert to being on the receiving end of indecency. The anticipation of being targeted by rude colleagues exacts a measurable toll on the ability to perform complex tasks requiring creativity, flexibility, and memory recall, according to another study by the University of Southern California's Marshall School of Business.[5] Verbal abuse affects more than just those who experience it directly. It can also harm innocent bystanders, suggests the authors in their study published in the *Academy of Management Journal*.

Rudeness, sarcasm, and cynicism in the boardroom primes dysfunctional outcomes, such as inappropriate aggression and a hostile workplace, elsewhere in the enterprise. Behaviors that lead to #MeToo moments often begin with unchallenged workplace rudeness. Employee engagement and teamwork suffer as colleagues intentionally avoid perpetrators, file grievances, quit, and generally spend less time working productively.

Rudeness, unless quickly interrupted, can hijack organizational effectiveness. Here's a three-step process for challenging rudeness on the factory floor, in the boardroom, or elsewhere:

1. **Model decency.** The contradiction to rudeness starts and ends with how leaders model interpersonal behaviors such as empathy, humility, patience, professionalism, and self-discipline.

2. **Call it when you see it.** It's tempting to ignore incivility from colleagues, but ignoring it just makes it worse. If you witness indecency from a subordinate or a peer, challenge it immediately. It's best to start with the offender personally, preferably in private, and without beating around the bush. Stick to the behavior and its consequences. The point is not to shame the offender, but to explain the negative impacts on the team that flow from rudeness. The offender will often try to minimize or offer what to him or her seems like justifications. Listen empathically but reject rationalizations. The message communicated without rudeness is that the rude behavior must stop. When the rudeness is from someone higher in power and status, the task becomes more difficult. It is best to recruit someone higher in authority to advocate for decency.

3. **Get a commitment and follow up.** Rudeness or bullying are learned behaviors; it takes effort and time to substitute new behaviors. Formalize the intervention. Get a commitment from the offender that he or she will honor standards of decency at work. Communicate clearly that there will be consequences for violations of the standards. Set targets, if appropriate. Put the agreement in writing. Ensure that violations have consequences. Accountability is the key.

Decency Role Models

Wegmans Food Markets is a $9.2 billion supermarket chain with 49,000 employees in 100 stores that is perennially honored as one of the top 100 great places to work in America. Founding president Robert Wegman was famous for instilling its now-famous rich, enabling culture.

Within the employee population at the headquarters flagship store, the founder of Wegmans was noted for his attention to individual employees. At one point, Wegman was puzzled by the behavior of one devoted, longtime employee (we'll call him Henry), a parking lot attendant who gathered the empty shopping carts and returned them to the store. Wegman knew Henry was loyal and pleasant to customers and employees alike, but he was puzzled that Henry never seemed to smile when he was greeted. After some discrete probing, Wegman learned why Henry didn't smile: He was embarrassed by having lost most of his teeth. He couldn't afford to go to the dentist. This was a secret that Wegman secretly fixed. Without Henry knowing his benefactor, an orthodontist was arranged, and Henry was all smiles thereafter.

Reuben Mark, the ex-CEO of Colgate-Palmolive, is a legend of humility and cultural sensitivity. Notoriously press-shy, he is as comfortable on a factory floor as he is with Wall Street analysts. He's known to joke with factory workers in Spanish. When a newly hired (from Dial Corporation) employee slipped him a copy of Dial's current marketing plan, Reuben's response was vintage Mark: He sent the sealed package unopened to Dial's CEO Herb Baum. Reuben led with honor.

Ken Iverson (1925–2002), former chairman of Nucor Corporation and author of *Plain Talk: Lessons from a Business Maverick*, is one of our heroes. The way he promoted employee engagement allowed Nucor to revolutionize the steel industry and run circles around its competitors. Iverson was a brilliant strategist, but we believe he succeeded because he understood how employee engagement leveraged Nucor's effectiveness. Iverson abhorred hierarchy and overhead. Even when Nucor's annual revenue approached $4 billion, the company operated from modest headquarters, with only four layers of management. He pushed authority and accountability close to the customer-facing workers. Iverson knew that by giving employees a stake in the business and turning them loose—by inspiring teamwork—Nucor would thrive.

Herb Kelleher (1931–2019), legendary founder and CEO of Southwest Airlines, was a poster child for decency at work. His death at age 87 as this book was being prepared saddened us, but his impact on the organizational culture of Southwest Airlines endures. Herb piloted the storied growth of "the airline that love built." His work made air travel a regular part of America's middle class. That culture was recognized as a model of employee empowerment. Herb established the annual "Top Wrench Award" for the maintenance crew and the "Top Cleaner" award acknowledging the efforts of those who may otherwise be lost in unglamorous but indispensable jobs.

We admired Kelleher for injecting the concept of "love" into employee culture, for eschewing standard corporate practices, and for his down-home business wisdom. We can think of no better way to honor his memory than to share some of our favorite Kelleher quotes.

On loyalty: "The core of our success. That's the most difficult thing for a competitor to imitate. They can buy all the physical things. The things you can't buy are dedication, devotion, loyalty—the feeling that you are participating in a crusade."

On strategy: "Think small and act small, and we'll get bigger. Think big and act big, and we'll get smaller."

On leadership: "Power should be reserved for weightlifting and boats. Leadership really involves responsibility."

On people: "Your employees come first. And if you treat your employees right, guess what? Your customers come back, and that makes your shareholders happy. Start with employees and the rest follows from that."

On humility: "You can't really be disciplined in what you do unless you are humble and open-minded. Humility breeds open-mindedness—and really, what we try to do is establish a clear and simple set of values that we understand. That simplifies things; that expedites things. It enables the extreme discipline I mentioned in describing our strategy. When an issue comes up, we don't say we're going to study it for two and a half years. We just say, 'Southwest Airlines doesn't do that. Maybe somebody else does, but we don't.' It greatly facilitates the operation of the company."

Indelible Stories

Decencies are indelible stories. Albert Schweitzer said, "The ideal in life is only in small part due to bold public action by important people. All the rest is made of small and obscure deeds." Sometimes, says author Joseph Badaracco, "It's the smallest acts that influence other people months or years later."

In their extensive research on employee engagement, the consultants at the Gallop Organization suggest this as the typical employee wish list: "Focus me, know me, care about me, hear me, help me feel proud, help me review my contributions, help me grow, help me build mutual trust, challenge me."[6] We would add: "Lead me with decency." And if the time comes to say goodbye, do it with class and civility, because leaders who are called on to terminate an employee are making a different kind of memory.

Living Decency

Dan Clarino has been the president of the award-winning Re/Max Benchmark Realty Group in his region of New York state for more than 25 years. He is an ex-Marine and Vietnam War vet who is the recipient of two purple hearts. Dan is also on the board of the regional Habitat for Humanity.

Dan has served as guardian on the biennial Honor Flights for World War II and Korean War vets who are honored for their service when they arrive to fanfare in our nation's capital. In addition, Dan cashes out military vets and police officers in restaurants and supermarkets; provides free lunch every week for all his agents, staff, and tenants in his office building; and handwrites at least five thank-you notes each week to deserving Re/Max employees throughout his organization.

In a refreshing departure from standard industry practice, Clarino refuses to let his agents wait for their commission check following a closing transaction. Years ago, Dan arranged for his agents to receive their commissions immediately after the transaction via direct deposit.

Netflix Culture Deck

If you want to experience how a world-class company articulates its vision and values, you can't do better than checking out the "Netflix Culture: Freedom & Responsibility" PowerPoint deck.[7] It's available on SlideShare. The 124-page presentation has been called the "the most important document ever to come out of [Silicon] Valley" by Facebook COO Sheryl Sandberg. The executive behind the presentation is Patty McCord, the former chief talent officer at Netflix. The common theme within the company's values is to treat employees as adults.

In practical terms, treating employees as adults translates into fewer policies, rules, and restrictions than any Fortune 500 company we are aware of. Netflix employees have no formal limits to vacation days. Travel policies are virtually nonexistent. There are no annual employee reviews. What Netflix wants to attract and retain are self-aware, self-sufficient, "fully formed adults" who agree to be accountable. "If we start with the assumption that everybody comes to work to do an amazing job, you'd be surprised what you get," McCord says. Highlights of the values articulated in the Netflix Culture Deck include:

The work of management is to build great teams and individuals, rather than to control people. When managers build great teams, they do amazing stuff.

People want to do work that means something. After they do it, they should be free to move on. Careers are journeys. Every employee who leaves becomes an ambassador for not only the product but also for who you are and how you operate.

Everyone in the company should be able to handle the truth. Humans can hear anything if it's true. Rethink the word "feedback," and think about it as telling people the truth, the honest truth, about what they're doing right and what they're doing wrong, in the moment when they're doing it.

Fringe on Top

Charles "Chip" Bell is an author, keynote speaker, and consultant in customer loyalty and service innovation. In a recent newsletter, he recounts the following story:

> I stopped at a grocery store in a small town on my drive to my remote river house for the weekend. Standing at the checkout counter, I watched as the check-out clerk bagged my groceries. Unexpectedly, she pulled from her uniform pocket a single bright-colored balloon and extended her hand. "I'll bet you are somebody's grandpa and you will put this to good use." I was stunned! My day just got enchantingly fringed!

As Bell explains, the "fringe on top" phrase originates from Rogers and Hammerstein's hit Broadway play *Oklahoma!* The cowboy Curly wins the attention of Laurey when he promises a ride to the box picnic social in "The Surrey with the Fringe on Top." The decorated carriage was a metaphor for adding magic to a moment, an action that breaks the humdrum of daily life. It is a random act that not only creates a special experience and memory, it beckons its recipient to return for more. There can be no better definition of a decency.

Bell suggests that all leaders can create such lasting memories through small gestures. "It demands initiative to make a difference in another person's life," he adds. "It requires valuing a whimsical moment that, like a Cracker Jack prize, might be financially worthless but emotionally priceless. Go forth and put your own fringe on top of the experiences you create every day."

Principal Financial Group

Dan Houston, CEO, president, and chairman of the board for the Principal Financial Group, Des Moines, Iowa, is a classic example of someone who's risen through the ranks. After joining the company in 1984 and through a series of promotions, he is recognized as both an industry leader and an involved and committed citizen. He is an example of leadership with an eye toward the near-impossible, making a big company feel culturally small. To that end, the company holds regular "town hall" meetings with employees. He's accessible to colleagues from boardroom to lunchroom. Dan is a tireless advocate of a multicultural environment, symbolized by eight separate, active employee committees.

During Principal's rare workforce reductions, Dan leads the effort to place or transfer employees to ensure income continuation. At-risk employees are given ample time to post for jobs internally and are given assistance in their external searches. He and the Principal leadership team are kept up to date on the success of jobs found. Dan is openly committed to "living Principal's values every day": ethical corporate governance, social responsibility, sustainability.

Baxter International

Baxter International is accustomed to being recognized for leadership excellence. If there were a national "above and beyond" award, CEO José Almeida would be a prominent honoree. The company has received the seal of approval from *CR Magazine* (Best Corporate Citizens), *Forbes* (Best Large Employers), the Workplace Gender Equality Agency's Employer of Choice for Gender Equality, The Human Rights Campaign, Diversity Best Practices, and The National Association of Female Executives. Baxter is also a member of the Dow Jones Sustainability Index. And somehow, Baxter has found time to perform financially and operationally while touching the lives of millions of people around the world every day. Baxter International's mission is simply this: save and sustain lives.

José Almeida believes that corporate governance sets the tone for an enduring culture. Committed as he is to advancing the diversity of Baxter's workforce, José has introduced "Gender IQ," the company's new leadership development program. Its focus: to bring heightened awareness to gender differences and its role to create a more productive and inclusive environment. He encourages all Baxter employees to sign the company's "All In(clusive)" workplace pledge, and Almeida's signature on PwC's "CEO Action for Diversity and Inclusion" pledge underscores this commitment.

José Almeida believes that Baxter's commitment to diversity and inclusion "fuels the company's ability to deliver on our ultimate mission: Save and sustain lives. . . . Corporate responsibility is an essential part of who we are."

The Lee Hecht Harrison Twinkle Awards

We can attest to how motivating a well-considered and highly personal employee recognition program can be. The Twinkle Awards grew out of its history of giving gifts as awards to colleagues at the annual Holiday Gala party—an event attended by colleagues and their spouses or guests. The original idea for the Twinkle Awards was inspired by an employee, Pat Pursley.

This was a program based on peer recognition rather than management acknowledgment. Colleagues were asked to nominate their peers for the Awards by completing this sentence: "(Name of coworker) is a Shining Star because . . ."

Each associate could nominate as many peers as they wanted. The nominations were anonymously placed in a big sparkly container in the middle of the office. When a

Twinkle Award nomination was put in the tub, a whistle was blown and a big "ta-da" was announced.

The results were amazing. The nominations were heartfelt, personal, and endearing. They showed the true affection, respect, and gratitude the department members felt for one another. Over the years, Twinkle Awards were given out at the Holiday Gala. The award was an ornament in the shape of a star as well as a dinner for two, courtesy of Lee Hecht Harrison. As each award was announced, the audience heard what their coworkers had written about the recipient.

Over the course of the program, everyone received a Twinkle Award. Everyone felt special, honored, and inspired. They recognized that everyone belonged to a fabulous group of people that shined together.

CHAPTER 7

EMPLOYEE ENGAGEMENT IN ACTION

> *"Can capitalism be made more decent and its instrument, business, work more obviously for the good of all everywhere?"*
> **—CHARLES HANDY**

How can we differentiate our organizations from all our competitors for the talent we are recruiting? By appealing to belief-driven candidates. We define belief-driven candidates as potential hires who believe companies and brands should take a stand on important issues. In other words, they should stand for a purpose.

Purposeful engagement can make all the difference in inspiring employees and teams to do great things. One attribute that gets the attention of top talent is the chance for meaningful work with a competent supervisor for a company that has a shared purpose. Engagement and purpose are the magnets for attracting top talent to an organization.

We have seen it with our own eyes. Disengaged employees who see little or no overall purpose in their work provide a fraction of the productivity and innovation compared to those who are aligned with the enterprise. Also, disengaged employees are more likely to be actively or passively seeking other jobs. Employee engagement, loyalty, and trust reliably promote organizational efficiency and success. Many companies need to significantly improve their employee engagement building skills.

There is a problem with employee engagement. Statistics from Gallup's 2017 State of the Global Workplace Report paint a bleak picture of corporate cultures.[1] These are the cultures that too often undermine leaders and talent managers who are responsible for creating the supportive and purposeful workplaces that make it possible to recruit and retain top talent. The following six statistics are indeed troubling.

1. **Eighty-five percent of employees worldwide are not engaged at work.** Gallup's 2017 State of the Global Workplace Report found that 85 percent of workers from around the world either are not engaged or are actively disengaged with their jobs. That's a huge number of employees who are uninspired and, therefore, less motivated to be innovative and productive. One solution: creating thoughtful employee development plans based on each employee's unique goals and passions.

2. **Seventeen percent of employees worldwide are actively disengaged.** Active disengagement is more than employees not putting forth the extra effort. We are talking about workers who have basically given up and are just phoning it in. Top performers tend to leave organizations that tolerate the presence of disengaged employees. In extreme cases, disengaged employees actually sabotage the mission. Much of this disengagement is the responsibility of the organization itself and its leaders. Employees aren't being nurtured, listened to, inspired, or appreciated.

3. **Fifty-seven percent of talent management professionals find it challenging to create engaging employee experiences in learning.** Research by SilkRoad in 2018 reveals that recruiters and HR specialists find it challenging to deliver great performance in recruiting (46 percent) and onboarding (41 percent).[2] Attracting great talent is a continual goal, but keeping that talent can be equally challenging, which is why an enabling organizational culture remains so critical for productivity and profitability.

4. **Thirty-three percent of employees want to leave their jobs because they're bored.** When Korn Ferry surveyed nearly 5,000 professionals and asked why they were planning on looking for a new job in the subsequent year, one-third checked "I'm bored, need a new challenge."[3] Employees who feel they are stagnating may disengage or, worse, may seek better opportunities

elsewhere. Improved employee development, including dynamic training programs, along with a sense of purpose, can give workers a reason to stay and be engaged.

5. **Thirty-two percent of employees who leave their jobs within 90 days do so because of company culture.** Jobvite's 2018 Job Seeker Nation Study uncovered that, amazingly, 30 percent of survey respondents have left their jobs within 90 days.[4] Nearly a third of those new hires who bolt within three months do so because the company culture is a problem. Aside from how expensive hiring is and how costly high attrition rates can be, the most startling aspect of this stat is that it shows that new hires can tell if a company culture is toxic almost immediately. Moreover, 15 percent of respondents turned down a job offer because of an organization's culture and reputation.

6. **Engaged employees make their organizations 17 percent more productive and 21 percent more profitable.** Great business leaders have always known what Gallup's report confirmed: engagement is beneficial not only for the employee but also for the entire organization. Taking active steps toward achieving that engagement leads to a workplace where employees feel valued, respected, and empowered to be creative. This provides two important benefits— employees feel a sense of purpose in the work they do and, in turn, that motivation inspires and encourages employees to seek out new initiatives within the organization to help it grow.

The job of leaders in the age of social good is to activate purpose. Undeniably, employee engagement matters. It affects everything critical to building a successful organization, from talent retention and career development to leadership development and workplace culture. However, the more frightening statistics we've highlighted, when taken seriously, can be catalysts for change, especially when a company experiences high attrition, loss of faith in leadership, and an overall lack of vision in the organization.

The Impact of Perks on Employee Engagement

Treating employees well pays off. The key is to ensure that the treatment employers offer is the treatment employees want. Tech companies, such as Apple, Google, Facebook, and Microsoft, have led the way in treating their employees to a variety of perks, ranging from free meals to onsite fitness centers. At the same time, these firms also innovated with flexible work schedules, generous vacation policies, and paid maternal and paternal leave. As these perks become normalized, other industries are slowly catching up.

Do any of these perks have a significant impact on employee engagement as measured by advantages in recruitment, retention, and employee motivation? And, if so, are the impacts limited to the United States, or can they be generalized to firms in other countries?

A new study of companies finds that treating employ-ees well does pay off. This study, based on Thomson Reuters's ASSET4 database, which references many aspects of workplace culture, analyzed data on employee relations and company performance on 3,500 organiza-tions in 43 countries from 2002 to 2014.[5] The research focused on eight dimensions that, in the aggregate, are meant to represent how well firms treat their employees. Under the study's framework, the eight dimensions of treating employees decently are:

- Employment quality. The study assigned a measure to the quality of a company's benefit packages and job conditions.
- Health and safety of the workplace.
- Training encompassing the company's commitment to providing development and educational opportunities for its workers.
- Workplace diversity, which includes equal opportunities for career advancement.
- Respect for human rights and labor laws.
- Diversity program—74 percent of the companies had one.
- Formal training program—62 percent provided skills training for their employees.
- Employee health and safety initiatives—55 percent established goals based around employee health and safety.

The bottom line is clear: treating employees well pays off. Companies with a higher Employee Friendly (EF) culture score reported higher performance numbers.[6] They tended to report better returns on both assets and equity relative to comparable firms scoring lower on the EF scale. Companies with stronger EF workplaces also reported better sales-to-assets ratios and lower expenditures. Companies high on EF reported fewer strikes. They filed more patents, a proxy for innovation.

Overall, the research is consistent with the hypothesis that treating employees well inspires higher levels of engagement, efficiency, and teamwork. "These results suggest that creating an EF culture is value-enhancing when managers make choices (including the creation of an EF culture) that are in line with shareholders' interests," according to research published in the *Journal of Corporate Finance*.[7]

Institutionalizing the Decency Code

So, what can be done? This section offers a blueprint for a program of employee engagement decencies designed to promote a culture of meaningful work and purpose designed to attract, recruit, and retain top talent.

Decencies are scalable. As decencies become more widespread—as they become something that institutions, not simply individuals, do—they tend to become perceived as more newsworthy. For that reason, it's pretty easy to look on company websites, in printed reports, or in the media to find examples of big decencies the companies or their observers find valuable. What we find most interesting are ideas that probably started as small decencies but have morphed into something institutional. The examples below are only a small sampling of big decencies in the workplace we've run across that deliver on some or all of the psychological needs of employees.

- **Southwest Airlines.** When it came time in 2014 for Southwest Airlines to create new uniforms for workers, instead of hiring an outside designer, the airline challenged the employees to do it. Everyone was encouraged to submit designs. Thousands of workers expressed interest. In the end, Southwest had 43 finalists. Despite having to pick one winner and leave 42 employees disappointed, the company had encouraged collaboration. Over the course of a year, selected employees met every two weeks to collaborate on the design of the new uniforms. The result? A bolder uniform as much functional as fashionable for employees. One participant called the exercise an "unforgettable experience."
- **Ritz-Carlton.** Every employee of a Ritz-Carlton hotel, from the concierge who speaks four languages to the housekeeper who cleans the rooms, has the authority, without manager involvement, to spend up

to $2,000 to solve a problem with a customer. Think about it: Any Ritz-Carlton employee can spend more money than some of them earn in a month to solve a customer problem.

Of course, the Ritz-Carlton hotels invest significantly in their employees. All recruits go through tests that screen them for the attributes of the most successful Ritz employees. Ritz has learned that applicants whose test scores resemble those of its most exemplary employees tend to succeed. After employees are hired, training/coaching is constant. The result is not surprising. The Ritz-Carlton brand stands for perhaps the best hotel experience in the world. Ritz-Carlton hotels are so legendary for their reliable level of customer service that the chain received the coveted Malcolm Baldrige National Quality Award. As customers, we may see a small decency when the bellhop gives us a bottle of water so that we can have something to drink during our taxi ride, but the gesture is, in reality, an expression of a big, programmatic decency.

- **Metso Minerals.** Many companies have mentoring programs. We think there is no better way to make new employees feel welcomed, comfortable, and effective from day one. Optimum results come when the mentors are volunteers, according to Dawna Smeltzer, manager of aftermarket services at Metso Minerals Industries. At her company, new employees shadow the mentor for six months after they are hired. The aim of the program is to facilitate skills transfer and to get the new employee integrated within the department and the company as effectively as possible. The company benefits in two broad ways. "First, new employees become productive much more quickly," Smeltzer says. The mentoring also contributes to a high retention level. Employees who are frustrated or having difficulties can often go to their mentor. Metso's turnover rate is much lower than the industry average. Second, the company benefits because the job shadowing is good for the mentor too.

- **Disney.** At Walt Disney World in Orlando, Florida, one of its 180 recognition programs is called "The Spirit of Fred Award," named for an employee named Fred. When Fred first went from an hourly to a salaried position, five people taught him the values necessary for success at Disney. This experience helped to inspire the award, and the name Fred became an acronym for Friendly, Resourceful, Enthusiastic, and Dependable. First given as a lark, the award has come to be highly coveted in the organization. There is also the Lifetime Fred Award—a bronze statuette of Mickey Mouse given to those who have won several Spirit of Fred Awards. Here, one employee's decency is elevated to a structured program that still retains a personal touch.

- **AT&T Universal Card Services.** The Jacksonville, Florida–based finance company uses the World of Thanks Award as one of more than 40 recognition and reward programs. It's a pad of colored paper shaped like a globe with "thank you" written all over it in different languages. Anyone in the company can write a message of thanks to someone else and send it to that person. The program is extremely popular; in four years the company has used more than 130,000 such notes. That's 130,000 small decencies rolled into one big decency program.

- **Office of Personnel Management.** The United States Office of Personnel Management in Washington, DC, uses a "pass around" award that was first given to the division's "special performer." Later that person passed the award to another person who, he/she believed, truly deserved it. The award came to take on great value and prestige because it came from one's peers. A recipient can keep the award as long as he or she wants, or until he or she discovers another special performer. When the award is to be passed on, a ceremony and lunch are planned.

- **Hewlett-Packard.** A Hewlett-Packard company engineer burst into his manager's office in Palo Alto, California, to announce he'd just found the solution to a problem the group had been struggling with for many weeks. His manager quickly groped around his desk for some item to acknowledge the accomplishment and ended up handing the employee a banana from his lunch with the words, "Well done. Congratulations!" (How's that for a spontaneous, no-cost gesture of appreciation? A smaller decency there never was.) The first employee so honored was understandably puzzled, but eventually the charm of the gesture proved irresistible. The next time someone did something noteworthy, people looked around for a banana. Over time the institutionalized Golden Banana Award became one of the most prestigious honors bestowed on an inventive employee.

- **East Alabama Medical Center.** East Alabama Medical Center allows employees and work groups to choose their own shifts. A hospital has to run 24 hours a day, seven days a week, including holidays, and that obligation creates an enormous scheduling burden for management. Some shifts are always more desirable than others. The Medical Center solves this problem in a unique way: Supervisors don't impose a schedule. Instead, workers come together, figure out what shifts have to be covered, and self-select to fill them out of a sense of community. By transferring responsibility for this challenging management process to the workers who are most affected by it, workers also take ownership of the task.

- **Crate and Barrel.** Crate and Barrel store managers in Houston began a program for their associates involving a "surprise hour off." Once a week, each store manager picks a sales associate and takes his or her shift on the floor for an hour saying, "You've been working hard, and I appreciate it. Enjoy a paid hour off. Come back refreshed and ready to sell more."

Decencies to Promote Employee Engagement

- **Start team meetings with appreciations.** Open team meetings with five minutes of appreciations, kudos, or expressions of gratitude during which leaders and team members can acknowledge great work of their colleagues.
- **Give 100 percent when you meet.** We get it. You're busy. We're all busy. But what signal does it send your followers when you are meeting with them while also answering your phone, checking e-mail, or responding to texts? This book is not the place to consider the supposed benefits of multitasking, but a meeting with followers is *not* the place to multitask.
- **Invite an employee to represent you at meetings.** For example, occasionally ask a team member to represent you at a status meeting. Of course, the employee has to be empowered to speak for you within limits. The trust has to be mutual.
- **Involve employees in strategic planning.** Make team members an active part of the planning process. Invite them to put their fingerprints on the future. Contributors are more likely to adopt what they help to create. Involve your team in planning ahead,

assessing opportunities, and coming up with ideas to improve your business strategy. The more employees feel invested in the process, the more engaged they will be in the process. Doing so promotes transparency and offers employees strategic insight into company operations. It fosters loyalty and builds a pipeline of better-prepared managers.

- **Build in "Intrapreneurship" Events.** Many talented millennials aspire to the start-up life. Organizations don't have to lose this talent if the employees can meet their entrepreneurship needs by creating opportunities for "intrapreneurship"; that is, encouraging employees to develop new enterprises and commercially viable ideas within the company. There are good models for this. 3M encourages all its engineers to devote one day a week to their own projects. Unilever has a start-up hub to keep bright ideas generated by its employees in-house. The key is to create an environment of validation where failure is never penalized.

  For example, in 2015, Rite-Solutions, a software developer, created the Mutual Fun platform. It combines social networking and gamification strategies to create a market for new innovation. Employees create personalized profiles to allow participants to discover others in the organization with similar interests and complementary strengths to work with on innovative projects. The teams then invest their intellectual capital (in the form of virtual US$10,000) into the "idea stocks" of the colleagues they would support. A leaderboard of teams is publicly posted.

- **Encourage peer-to-peer recognition programs.** Companies can build recognition into their business practices by creating peer-to-peer recognition programs in which employees are provided monthly reward points that they can give away to colleagues for work-related wins. Employees who earn a certain number of points can redeem them for various perks, such as a restaurant gift card or an extra personal day. Peer-to-peer recognition can eliminate a dynamic common to many companies: the perception that some contributors were getting benefits because they were more "liked" by supervisors. One way to address this issue is to create programs in which employees are invited to nominate their peers for recognition. The companies that tried this found themselves in a better position to retain high-value client business as a direct result of more engaged customer-facing employees.

- **Involve employees in the hiring process.** They don't want to be just another check-the-box interview. Give them a vote or even a veto. Involve them in the actual decision making about who joins the team. And while you're at it, involve them in creating the onboarding experience. Maybe it will be a self-guided onboarding exercise or other innovative solution. Set the ground rules and give them basic instructions, a list of objectives, and a time frame; for example, a 45-day plan, with some basic milestones.

- **Crowdsource the CSR.** As we have seen, workers
  today want their employers to be part of the social
  justice movement. To their credit, many companies
  respond by making substantial charitable donations
  to the communities in which they operate as part of
  the corporate social responsibility umbrella. While
  that's good, wouldn't it be better if the beneficiaries
  of that philanthropy were determined not by some
  obscure committee but by the employees themselves?
  It's easy. Ask every team member to make a pitch
  for their favorite charity and then have a fair process
  to distribute the available resources in a way that's
  agreeable to the team. This process can distribute
  cash or gifts and can result in more employee
  involvement. Giving time can be more rewarding
  than giving money, especially for Gen Y employees,
  who are highly oriented toward social involvement.
  Commit to taking action; this is how engagement
  happens.

In an age of commoditization, many companies are
look-alikes, virtually indistinguishable from each other in
terms of salaries, benefits, and working conditions. Belief-
driven candidates are rewarding companies and brands
they believe in. On average, companies such as Starbucks,
Ben & Jerry's, and Dove that deliver a conspicuous purpose connection with their employees and customers are
growing 30 percent faster.

Decencies and Great Places to Work

Michael C. Bush, CEO of Great Place to Work, is an expert on great companies. The trick, it turns out, is not so much in attaining greatness but in sustaining it. We asked Michael to weigh in on the imperative of decencies on the formula of great companies. This is what he reports:

> As CEO of Great Place to Work, I get to hear inspiring stories of leaders and organizations every day. Many of them are about the ways people treat each other with decency, fairness, and humility as they work to create what we call a Great Place to Work For All. By that, we mean a culture that maximizes the human potential of everyone in the organization, no matter who they are or what they do.
>
> Our research has found that when you've got a Great Place to Work For All, it's better for your business results, better for your people, and better for the world. And for organizations to make our lists of Best Workplaces—including the annual 100 Best Companies to Work For list we publish with Fortune—their employees must tell us through our Trust Index® survey that indeed their company has a consistently great culture for everyone.

Here are some highlights from the top ranking companies of the 100 Best Companies to Work For 2019 list:

Hilton Worldwide

#1 Fortune 100 Best Company to Work For, 2019

380,000 employees worldwide

Some of the nicest cafés at hotel giant Hilton are ones you can't get to as a guest. They are cafés for the hotel's own workers. Several years ago, Hilton upgraded its staff cafeterias and lounge spaces to make them as welcoming and comfortable as those visited by the hotel's guests. This investment is part of a push by CEO Chris Nassetta and other leaders to treat employees at every level as well as Hilton treats customers. And what Hilton calls the "Hospitality For All" culture is working.

Many organizations struggle to create a workplace environment that is equally great for frontline, hourly staff as it is for executives. With 380,000 team members worldwide, Hilton stands out for a consistently positive experience for its team members—no matter their job role. Through an inclusive purpose embraced by company executives, innovative programs, and effective leadership at every level of the organization, Hilton has achieved a Great Place to Work For All.

Chris Nassetta began in the hotel industry at the bottom, working as a maintenance staffer at a Washington, DC, Holiday Inn while on summer break from college. This included the thankless work of unclogging guest room toilets. What he remembers most from those summer gigs was the way his coworkers treated him as family despite his youth and part-time status. This included a farewell party complete with a gold-painted plunger as a parting gift!

Nassetta always reminds himself of what it's like to work on the front lines. At Hilton, he began an "immersion" program requiring Hilton execs to spend a week working in roles such as housekeeper, dishwasher, or bellhop. Nassetta himself took a turn as a maintenance team member in the Capital Hilton in Washington, DC. His coworkers there repeated the funny, warm send-off Nassetta experienced years before as a summer intern. "When I left," he recalls, "they gave me a golden plunger."

Wegmans Food Markets

#3 Fortune 100 Best Company to Work For, 2019
47,900 employees

An important way to treat employees decently is to listen to their ideas. One of the companies that does this best is grocery store chain Wegmans Food Markets. The Rochester, New York–based company consciously turns the typical organization hierarchy on its head, viewing leaders as servants in the servant-leadership model to the employees who directly serve customers. That translates into actively seeking out suggestions and new product ideas from employees stocking shelves, working cash registers, and cooking up sample meals for shoppers. Collaboration counts.

One of those meal coaches is Jody Wood. The way Wegmans listened to her has made a big difference to her, to the company, and to its customers. In 2014, Wood was seeking healthier food options for her husband. He was an insulin-dependent diabetic. His mobility had decreased to the point that he couldn't walk up or down his driveway.

While talking to a Wegmans customer, though, Wood learned of an alternative, veggie-focused diet described in the book *The End of Diabetes*. That led her to discover "cauliflower rice"—a minced-up version of cauliflower that can substitute for regular rice but has only one-ninth of the carbs that the body turns into sugar.

Wood loved the stuff and suggested to her coworkers and managers that Wegmans sell it. Wegmans leaders agreed to test it. It was a hit in Wood's Bridgewater, New Jersey, Wegmans. Soon after, the company began producing and selling cauliflower rice throughout its 100 or so stores. Cauliflower rice proved to be a godsend to Wood's husband. Thanks to a low-starch diet, he now walks two to four miles a day. The product also doubled sales of cauliflower at Wegmans, keeping it on the cutting edge of healthy foods.

At one point, company chairman Danny Wegman visited Wood's cook station. She told him her story, including how the book had inspired her. The next day he had Wood's manager put *The End of Diabetes* next to her cook station. Wood now touts the diabetic-friendly diet to customers. "It changes people's lives for the better, and they become healthier and happier," she says. "There's nothing worse than not feeling good. And there's nothing better than being healthy."

Workday

#4 Fortune 100 Best Company to Work For, 2019
6,700 employees

People of different generations have different priorities and needs, which creates challenges for a company trying to treat all their people with decency. One of the companies that best manages the complexity of a multigenerational workforce is business software company Workday.

The company has anchored its culture in research on generational differences, says Greg Pryor, Workday's senior vice president and "People and Performance Evangelist." Pryor says Workday accounts for millennials' "psychological narrative" that they must constantly expand their skills and social ties or they might lose their competitiveness and fail in life. The company also takes note of Gen Y's "gameful mindset" of seeking to acquire experiences so they can "level up" to the next opportunity, as they might in a video game.

These principles served as a backdrop to Workday's performance review process, Pryor says, which was rolled out in 2018. Called "Performance Enablement," it is less an annual, backward-looking ritual than a mechanism for giving continuous feedback and arranging "career sprints" of a few months at a time that lead to new skills and relationships.

"This generation is collecting—almost like you would collect in a backpack—different capabilities, different connections," Pryor says. "Capabilities are the new career currency given the mindset and narrative of millennials." All this work on millennials is paying off for Workday. Fully 96 percent of millennial employees at Workday say it is a great place to work, according to 100 Best Companies to Work For employee survey.

This progress has come from sometimes-hard conversations. Pryor recalls explaining how not getting frequent feedback amounts to a threat to millennials and how his comment prompted a revealing exchange. "One of our senior leaders, a Gen Xer, said, 'If I don't get feedback, that's a good thing. If I get feedback, you're telling me to get ready to get laid off.' That's the narrative from that generation," Pryor says. "This woman, who happened to be about 24 or 25, who was on our team raised her hand. She said, 'I just left a job because I didn't get feedback. Because I thought they didn't care about me.'"

The Trade Desk

#2 in Best Workplaces in Technology, 2019
900 employees

Sometimes the best way to treat people with decency is to remove people who don't treat others decently.

We see this at the best workplaces. They care so much about creating a great environment for everyone that they will let go of employees who disrespect others, even if the person mistreating peers or subordinates is a top performer in other respects. Consider this story we heard from Jeff

Green, CEO and founder of advertising technology firm The Trade Desk.

Green had an operations executive whose performance was excellent. But members of her team of roughly a dozen people began complaining. It took Green some time to figure out whether the leader was just holding them to a high standard or if she was treating them poorly. It was the latter, he concluded. He also determined that the problem wasn't curable. So even though the exec was getting some of the best results in the entire business and was someone he cared about, Green asked her to leave his 906-person Ventura, California–based company.

"It was one of the toughest conversations I've had," Green recalled. But he also said the short-term pain of losing a top performer he liked was worth the long-term gain of replacing her with a leader who could allow the company to grow. "It's critical to the culture, but it's also critical to the ongoing business," Green said. "I needed her to be a manager of over 30 people if she were here today. There's no way that can exist with the caliber of people we want on the team if she treats them like that."

The decision reflected Green's vision of the company as family. Even as his global team works to apply cutting-edge data science and stock trading principles to the digital advertising market, Green believes in an old-fashioned notion of an organization as a close-knit unit. "We're building something of a home," he said. "This is where we live. And this is where we want to be for a long time."

Engaging Millennial Workers

A word about millennials. Some people have suggested that millennial workers are engaged by a unique set of drivers. Our experience is that any worker, by and large, resonates to similar themes of decency-inspired engagement. Countless studies have considered why millennials are so different and why that difference makes them so unhappy at work.[8] We believe that the similarities between millennials and say, Gen X workers overwhelm the differences. Both demographics want to show up at work in their full selves and contribute to a mission that gives them meaning.

That said, it's worthwhile for leaders to consider the differences in what drives millennials to excel. Beyond that, we suggest it's more effective for leaders to celebrate the unique gifts of millennials and to be open to transforming the workplace to accommodate their interests in diversity and inclusion. This is a much better approach than trying to interpret generational differences and changing millennials to fit into established structures.

It would be the ultimate understatement to suggest that over the past 15 to 20 years, a lot has been spoken, written, lectured, and debated about the multigenerational workforce in the broader context of workplace diversity. Are millennials really that different from the generations before them? Yes and no. Is this an ageist rhetoric that's hurting your organization? Absolutely.

As noted by Greg Hammill, director of student programs at Fairleigh Dickinson University Silberman College of Business, "This is the first time in America's history that we have four different generations working side-by-side in the workplace. To begin to understand how individuals from different generations act and react, one must first start with understanding oneself. Begin by seeing where you fall on the generation timeline. This timeline represents a conglomeration of many views, starting and ending dates. Birth years of the generations are subjective, not scientific or agreed-on time spans. This subjectivity poses no real problem since the variation of years is not significant enough to impact the big picture of a generation's description. The first thing to consider is the individual and his or her underlying values or personal lifestyle characteristics."

A different insight comes from Peter Capelli of the Wharton School, University of Pennsylvania: "The problem older applicants often face is that younger supervisors don't want to hire them because they may not know how to manage them."

Just to review, today's employees are loosely seen as falling into these broad groups:

- **Boomers** (born 1946–1964), like the older veterans, value hard work and are often self-defined by work; they are success-oriented, title-focused, less likely to job-hop.

- **Generation Xers** (born 1965–1980) tend to be more self-reliant, less loyal, more tech-savvy, concerned with work-life balance, intrapreneurial, resourceful.
- **Millennials** (born 1980–2000) are most concerned about personal fulfillment (meaningful work), professional and career development, corporate responsibility, ethical leadership, teams, remote work options, multitasking, tech tools, recognition.
- **Generation Z** (born 2000+) are extremely tech-savvy, ambitious, culture-focused, team-oriented, entrepreneurial, creative.

The Case for Millennials and Gen Zs

The dismal statistics on employee engagement that we presented in Chapter 2 are even more pronounced among millennials who are increasingly taking over the workplace. Millennials are on pace to account for 75 percent of the US labor market by 2025. Millennials are tech-savvy, adaptable, and passionate about making a difference. They enter the workforce with enthusiasm as well as a unique set of expectations. Rarely, so far, are today's corporations equal to the task of living up to those expectations. The consequences are not pretty.

America's senior executives, most of whom are baby boomers nearing retirement, often chafe at the work habits of millennials. Stereotypes such as entitled, disloyal, lazy, impatient, and snowflake are thrown around. Some executives believe it is the job of their organizations to train millennials to fit into their longstanding organizational traditions and cultures. We believe that is an effort doomed to failure. The better approach is to find creative ways to leverage the unique priorities, perspectives, and purposes that energize millennials to transform the company's culture for the better. In the process, leaders will experience innovation, drive engagement, and cultivate the next generation of leaders.

Call it the loyalty challenge. Millennials, it is true, can tend to express limited loyalty to their current employers, although they often have great loyalty to their teammates and the common goal. It is also true that many are just one disappointment at work away from quitting. Many millennials are entrepreneurial. According to the 2016 Deloitte Millennial Survey, in any given year, one in four millennials are preparing to quit to join a start-up.[9] That figure increases to 44 percent when the time frame is expanded to two years. Only 16 percent of millennials see themselves with their current employers for as much as a decade. The study surveyed 4,300 millennials in more than 10 countries.

When they quit, it's often because they are disappointed. The disappointments often flow from insufficient alignment between the social values a company claims to have and the values it actually practices. Millennials insist that companies not only talk but also walk their values. Millennials often put their personal values ahead of organizational goals, and it's quite common to see them reject employers and assignments that conflict with their beliefs.

What Do Millennials Want?

What is it, exactly, that millennials want? The *Millennial Impact Report*, a recent study by Achieve Consulting, suggests some of the workplace behaviors that millennials exhibit.[10] Mostly, millennials want an opportunity to do work on their terms, be productive, have good supervision, and have the opportunity to make a difference in the world. Let's look at specifics. While all employees want some of these elements, millennials tend to rank some workplace dynamics higher than previous generations.

- **Teamwork above all.** Millennials prefer to work in teams with a constant state of collaboration. It's all about capturing and fueling a millennial behavior of team over individual to drive success.
- **Quality supervision.** Millennials often rank quality time with their manager at the top of the list of things they want in a workplace. Millennials want to see individualized focus and attention on their personal career path. They also want their manager to be an advocate for them in alleviating any workplace issues or concerns. Having regular one-on-one time with managers is key. Millennials want to feel they are being coached. They want mentors. They want to feel that their managers are their champions and that their individual interests are as important to their managers as the interests of the organization.
- **Flexible work arrangements.** Millennial employees look for flexibility. One proxy for that

is the opportunity to work from anywhere. While millennials welcome collaboration, they also understand that every job requires some heads-down time. When they need to focus, millennials want to be able to choose where to work. Millennials tend to chafe at restrictions such as fixed hours, sick days, vacations, etc. They want to be accountable for getting the work done, not monitored for how and when they work.

- **To be part of the decision.** If they don't know the why, millennials find it hard to stay engaged. "Because I said so" is never acceptable. This need to know the "why" behind everything makes millennials good employees but can also be extremely frustrating for managers. It's easy for boomer supervisors to suspect millennials of resistance to their authority or insubordination. Millennials want the big picture, the 10,000-foot view of everything. If managers keep millennials in the loop on the entire scope of any project they may be working on, the organization will benefit from highly productive workers instilled with a global business mindset.

- **Focus on career development.** For millennials, career progression is dominant. Failure to put in place programs to develop the careers of millennials will cause them to leave. In fact, 71 percent of millennials say they're likely to leave their company within two years. The only way to arrest such turnover is to offer enriching career development opportunities. There is no other way. Throwing money at the individuals by itself won't solve the problem. This is the talent with the most options.

Millennials vote with their feet. It's a truism in the HR profession that employees don't leave their jobs, they leave their managers. Unfortunately, too many millennials are justified in concluding that their skills aren't being developed by their managers. About a quarter of millennials say that senior managers are the greatest barrier to innovation. Taken together, many millennials feel traditional command-and-control leadership structures are holding them back.

If millennials stay engaged, it's because they see concrete evidence that their managers are rooting for them and the organization is structured for their growth. The solution must be a career development plan that is tailored and specific to the interests and passions of every contributor. Does this require extra effort from HR, the managers, and the entire organization? Of course. No two conversations will be the same. But that's appropriate because no two contributors are the same. It's nevertheless critical for managers to continue to open up these conversations with employees so that workers feel invested in and valued, which will inevitably lead to higher engagement. The investment has handsome payoffs in terms of innovation and breakthrough performance. Business leaders are in the driver's seat to foster this process to increase engagement.

- **Fast career progression.** The stereotypical complaint with millennials is that they are impatient. Maybe. It's not unusual for millennials to welcome lateral career moves in pursuit of career satisfaction. Money is not as much of a motivator for millennials as many managers might think. A recent study by Cornerstone OnDemand found that the biggest motivator for changing positions is the promise of purpose and fulfillment, not money.[11] Millennials are impatient with timetables and paying dues. Millennials also want real-time, specific feedback. In return, they are eager to learn new skills and will work hard to become even more valuable to the company. On the other hand, millennials value mobility. If they are not satisfied, they are quick to quit. A 2015 study by the Education Advisory Board suggests that millennials will job hop up to 20 times in their career, about twice as many times as their baby boomer counterparts.[12]

- **Continuous feedback.** All employees want feedback about their performance. Millennials demand it. It's a form of psychic income. How appropriate, then, that the word "feedback" starts with the word "feed." Without feedback not only from managers but also from teammates and even the customers they serve, millennials feel malnourished. The lack of lively and timely feedback impoverishes employees. Millennials are content to spend 40, 50, or even more hours at work, dedicating their energies to the enterprise. Getting feedback on their efforts is not much to ask. Yet as study after study shows, most employees want more specific and timely feedback than the organization is prepared to offer.[13] Managers say they have no time. But they have time to make excuses. The reality is that it is sometimes uncomfortable to offer specific feedback and, to be fair, some employees resist receiving it. But managing is what managers get paid to do. Withholding feedback can lead to stunted growth, lack of clarity, loss of talent, missed opportunities, and, of course, disengagement.

- **Recognize and appreciate.** Employee engagement isn't about what your employees can do for you, but what you can do for your employees to motivate them. Beyond conversations and programs about career development comes continual recognition and appreciation of individual and team efforts. We know that informal peer recognition is often as important as formal recognition. While cash awards are appropriate, millennials also value symbolic rewards that capture the passion of the effort. Millennials often value experiences, such as a company-paid holiday, over awards of cash.

- **Fixing problems, not symptoms.** Millennials resist projects that look like applying Band-Aids to problems. They want to bite into the problem itself, not waste time on fixing symptoms. Millennials want to feel valued, and the best way to express that value is by giving them a crack at solving real problems.

- **A social work environment.** Many millennials look for a social environment at work. On one level, they value office activities and socializing where they can get to know their coworkers better. On another, they want to have an impact on the world and for the company to support specific values around issues such as social justice, inclusivity, and environmental sustainability. Millennials value volunteer days where the whole office gets together and spends time outside of the office in the service of some social good.

The leader's challenge: to be agile enough to lead a culture where half of the employees believe in bosses and budgets and half believe in visions and values!

CHAPTER 8

DECENCY WHEN IT'S TIME TO SAY GOODBYE

"Every exit is an entry somewhere else."

—TOM STOPPARD

ere's the reality: Most laid-off individuals can come to terms with the fact that separations are a fact of work life in today's dynamic business environment. But what they have not, and should not have to come to terms with is a downsizing that is mismanaged through lack of preparation, insensitivity, or neglect of human dignity and respect.

In *Business: The Ultimate Resource*, a compilation of essays by the editors of Perseus Press, management psychologist Alan Downs proposes that layoffs are an engagement factor. "Downsizing is often executed with a brisk, compassionless efficiency that leaves laid-off employees angry, and surviving employees feeling helpless and demotivated," Downs says.

Helplessness is the enemy of employee engagement. It produces a work environment of withdrawal, risk-averse decisions, severely impaired morale, and excessive blaming. All these put a stranglehold on organizations that, in this economy, desperately need to excel. "How you treat people really matters—to the people who leave and the people who remain," warns Downs. If layoffs are inevitable, treating departing employees with dignity and decency will go quite a distance inside and outside the office.

To many people, job loss is the equivalent of divorce, even death, because of how intimately we identify ourselves with what we do for a living. For that reason, outplacement consultants find that at times it will feel as if they save lives. At their best, they are transfer-of-strength agents, transferring their strength to temporarily strength-depleted people—people who have lost not only their jobs but also an essential element of their identity. The job seekers have lost not only their salary income but their psychic income as well.

To some, the loss of their job threatens their reason for being. Separated people can slip into depression, self-destructive behavior, and, more rarely, violence targeted at others. In many cultures, the risk of suicide associated with job loss is well known. In Japan, for example, it is estimated there may be as many as 90 suicides per day, many related to workplace stress and job loss. That risk of serious trauma following job loss is partly what gave birth to the outplacement industry.

The Art of the Layoff

Many companies do everything in their power to avoid layoffs. Sometimes, however, economic realities make that impossible. When layoffs are imminent, small decencies can make a difference. A simple managerial commitment to small decencies during and immediately following a layoff does nothing to interfere with the economic necessities that forced the layoff. Small decencies put into play during and after this most difficult of management tasks—the act of separating an employee—will signal a leader's sensitivity and caring, and a commitment to everyone who is watching. And here's a critical point: everyone is watching and listening during and immediately after a downsizing.

This is no time for managerial myopia. Employees may be separated, but it's not so easy to erase the memory. "Survivor's guilt" is a real issue that can be managed, but only if it is acknowledged. So, also, must retained employees face the soul-crushing questions—"Am I next?" and "Is it over?"—that preoccupy retained employees after a downsizing. The use of the word "survivor" by a culture to describe the state of people still employed after layoffs underscores the life-and-death stakes at work. Ignoring the fact that the retained employees have been affected can result in long-lasting adverse impact on productivity and morale.

Layoffs may be inevitable. But when they are necessary, leaders who aspire to decency keep the following points in mind, as recommended by Guy Kawasaki, formerly chief evangelist of Apple and the author of *The Art of the Start*:

- **Take responsibility.** Some managers who inform employees that they are being separated are acting on instructions from a superior. Nevertheless, it is disempowering for the manager delivering the layoff notice to hide behind some version of "Don't blame me, I'm just the messenger." As true as that statement may be on some level, it evades responsibility and makes it easier for the firing manager to act callously. Invoking such boogeymen as competition, globalization, market conditions, or whatever macro forces can be blamed also evades responsibility. It's usually two people in a room plus a witness.

- **Cut deep and cut once.** Some leaders believe that economic conditions will get better soon, so they lay off the smallest number of people in anticipation of a miracle. Often the miracle doesn't materialize, and the company ends up making multiple cuts. Multiple layoffs are more demoralizing than one layoff.

- **Timing is everything.** One hour after the management team discusses the need to lay off employees, Kawasaki notes, the entire company will know that something is happening. "Once people know a layoff is coming, productivity drops like a rock. You're either laying people off or you're not—leaders should avoid the state of 'considering' a layoff."

- **Whack "Freddy."** For Kawasaki, "Freddy" represents the relative, friend, or friend of a friend that everyone knows was hired as a favor to the CEO or top executive. Freddies are often marginal employees who seem protected from accountability. When a layoff occurs, all eyes will be on what happens to "Freddy." Did Freddy survive the cut, or was his job eliminated? Cronyism has no place in a corporate culture that aspires to decency.

- **Share the pain.** According to Kawasaki, when employees are losing their jobs, the decent thing for leaders to do is to be sure the termination is aligned with other cost-containment moves. That might mean retiring the corporate jet, moving to smaller offices, turning in the company cars. Flying coach. Staying in motels. Give away the box tickets to the ball game. Give your 30-inch flat-panel display to a programmer who could use it to debug code faster. Do something, however symbolic.

- **Provide support.** Often marketplace conditions, or the people getting laid off aren't at fault. It can be the by-product of misguided policies from top management. There is a logic to providing services such as job counseling, résumé writing assistance, and job search help. There are firms that specialize in helping employees during "transitions."

It's Never Over

Leaders confront their own challenges during layoffs. Survivors of a downsizing typically harbor two questions: "Is it over?" and "Am I next?" Understandably, the instinct of leaders is to reassure. Leaders should resist this temptation. Leaders should tell the truth, even if the hard truth is not what survivors want to hear. "It is never over," says David Noer in *Healing the Wounds*. "This is as close to a law as anything I have found in the study of layoffs. The forces of the economy, the dynamics of technology, and the reality of the new employment contract make any kind of long-range employment promise an illusion."

Rather than avoid the virtual watercooler, managers should be visible, accessible, and forthright. Some language that we find appropriate for this situation includes: "We hope and expect that it's over. We'll do everything possible to avoid a repeat episode. But to promise otherwise risks conveying long-term false hope. Our priority now is to commit ourselves to a productive and successful future."

A Role Model for Layoffs

One of the best ways to learn about separation decencies is to examine how other companies have approached layoffs. Some stories serve as role models; others give us warnings. One of the better-managed downsizings of the past few years was undertaken in 2001 by Agilent, an $8.3 billion spin-off of Hewlett-Packard. The company was faced with an economic downturn that hit the telecom industry especially hard. Agilent had inherited much of the full employment culture of Hewlett-Packard, an organization that had never had a layoff. This heritage made what Agilent had to do especially difficult. After postponing the inevitable by belt-tightening, slashing expenses, and even getting employees to accept a temporary 10 percent, across-the-board salary cut, Agilent was forced to eliminate 4,000 jobs—9 percent of the company. But chairman emeritus Ned Barnholt laid out three ground rules:

1. Employees were to be notified only by their direct managers.
2. Managers would be clear and honest.
3. Layoff decisions were to be based on published criteria.

Barnholt understood that the downsizing campaign had to be two parts communication to one part implementation. On August 20, 2001, the day Agilent would report a quarterly loss of $219 million—its first loss ever—Barnholt got on the public address system for the first time, according to a report in *Fortune*, to tell employees about the loss before telling Wall Street.[1] Tradition was to be broken that day, and another tradition was to be created. Barnholt insisted on making the announcement to employees himself so they wouldn't have to hear about it from the media. He presented the deteriorating state of the business, recognized the sacrifices employees had already made, and detailed how many people would lose their jobs, where the number came from, and how the admittedly painful process would work.

This direct personal announcement was a decency that started the process on the right foot. Going forward, Agilent made the process as transparent as possible, demonstrating another separation decency: The forms managers were to use in making selections were posted on Agilent's intranet. Employees could see the criteria used as the basis for the selection decisions. Agilent considered the layoff regrettable but nothing to be ashamed about. Rarely has such a large organization been as public with a layoff as was Agilent.

The second round of communications was to come from the managers actually making the difficult decisions. Barnholt sent more than 3,000 managers through a series of daylong training exercises, where they role-played and practiced the right and wrong ways to separate people. Managers were expected to be as honest as possible. The company wanted a maximum of fairness and a minimum of ambiguity in the process and, by all accounts, it succeeded. Many of the employees Agilent separated wrote Barnholt that they were satisfied with the fairness and decency, if not the outcome, of the process.

Preparation, Preparation, Preparation

Separating an employee is too sensitive a situation to be handled without extensive advance planning. The entire episode, whether large or small scale, needs to be choreographed thoughtfully. This is not a time for a manager to be spontaneous. Managers do best when they receive separation training like that used at Agilent in the days immediately before the event. In these training sessions, managers learn what not to say, what to say, and how to say it. Managers are taught how to respond to an employee's emotional expressions, which can be intense. In essence, the training helps the manager behave decently even when the employee, understandably, may not.

No downsizing is perfect. There is often an inadvertent misstep, especially with large-scale workforce reductions, no matter how well planned. If there are 50 things that can go wrong in any downsizing and you think of 25 of them, you're a genius. But the one you miss can be devastating. That's why we are obliged to try to eliminate every opportunity for unnecessary missteps even though it is very difficult. Here are just a few examples of the avoidable mistakes.

Some years ago an enterprise with factories and branch offices throughout the United States was planning a major downsizing. The downsizing impacted thousands of workers in dozens of states across the country. The company, headquartered in an eastern state, did meticulous planning to have resources in place for those employees to be separated as well as for surviving employees when the downsizing announcement was made at 10 a.m. Unfortunately, the planners forgot that when it's 10 a.m. in Eastern Standard Time, it's 7 a.m. in Pacific Standard Time. Employees in the western states heard the news before they came to work and hours before the branch offices were ready. Confusion and hard feelings could have been avoided.

In another case, we thought we had sufficiently trained and coached the terminating manager about how to break the news that an employee was losing his job. But when the time came, the terminating manager couldn't quite bring himself to utter the appropriate words clearly enough. He obviously failed to deliver the message because the individual who was to be separated returned to the job the following morning! There is a natural human tendency to avoid confrontation, so it's understandable that we pull back from using direct language. That's why training and coaching are imperative.

In a third case, news of the upcoming layoff leaked out. This can be a real problem for an organization. If individuals learn of their upcoming separation through the newspaper, they are likely to have bitter feelings and may not even show up for their termination meetings. If local reporters get the story only from the voices of the separated employees, the company looks unprofessional and needs to do hurry-up damage control.

Avoid Creating the Most Obvious Pain and Suffering

Failing to be thoughtful about the day selected for the separation creates another set of avoidable mistakes. All it takes is a phone call to avoid separating an employee:

- On his or her birthday, especially before a milestone birthday (e.g., the day before the employee's fiftieth birthday)
- On a significant date such as the day before his or her pension plan vests
- On a religious holiday (e.g., Christmas, Easter, Yom Kippur, Ramadan)

- When the separation documents are not in order
- When a company activity could interfere with the scheduled event (e.g., "Bring Your Kid to Work Day")

3M, the company that developed Post-it Notes, has been celebrated for its innovative brand. When business realities made it necessary for 3M to cut 2,000 employees around the world, the company proceeded thoughtfully with a view toward reassuring its remaining employees. Remaining employees want to know their colleagues are taken care of. Managers need to assure the remaining staff that the separating employees are valued and that the organization is supporting them in the transition. Managers need to remain highly visible in the few months following a layoff. Closed door meetings invite speculation.

David Noer, author of *Healing the Wounds*, tells the story of a major company that embarked on a downsizing that resulted from a downturn in the company's fortunes. On the day of the downsizing, management neglected to check on something that unnecessarily rubbed salt into already open wounds. As the separated employees were leaving the building carrying boxes of their belongings, they saw contracted landscape specialists at work redesigning the corporate lawn. The separated employees had just been told that economic belt-tightening required their separation. Imagine the resentment on the part of the departing employees as they saw hundreds of thousands of dollars being spent on the corporate grounds. This situation could easily have been avoided.

An employee being separated is always a bad day for that employee. Some days and times are better than others. Fridays are ill-advised for a number of reasons. If corporate help such as outplacement is offered, it is usually not available on weekends. The employee separated on Friday has all weekend to stew without professional support. Experience shows that some employees separated on Fridays make tactical mistakes, such as panicking and firing off ill-considered e-mails or résumés. Sometimes family dynamics suffer when separated employees have too little support and too much time on their hands.

Avoid Mondays for a little-understood reason. Timing the notification on a Monday means that the managers have two days to forget the briefings they presumably received the prior week. Give a difficult process every chance to work. All things considered, the optimum days for separating employees are Tuesdays, Wednesdays, or Thursdays.

Where the conversation takes place is also important. The terminating manager's office may seem natural, but it presents a number of problems. First, if the employee being terminated gets visibly agitated or needs some time for composure, there is no place for the employee to regroup. For the manager to leave his or her own office so the separated employee can regain his or her composure is not practical or helpful.

Forcing a shaken and embarrassed employee to walk the gauntlet past coworkers is ill-advised on a number of levels. If the separated employee's coworkers do not know what happened, they may make an embarrassing mistake, such as engaging the person in a work conversation. If they do know, the hallway passing of the separated employee will be as uncomfortable for them as for the individual. In general, it's best to give the news in the separated employee's office or a vacant office. These locations also make it convenient for outplacement consultants or other supportive individuals to join the employee immediately after the notification.

Firing an employee in the company parking lot can make for a long-lasting bitter taste. Similarly, severing an employment relationship at a bar or restaurant will have a counterproductive effect. Both are too public, and neither provides the environment for the notifying manager to behave with decency and sensitivity.

Thoughtful companies also consider the employee's logistical issues, such as transportation. Many companies encourage carpooling. But if the employee to be separated is a member of a carpool, there are two issues that must be considered. First, will the employee want to ride with others on this difficult day? Second, if the employee is expecting to ride with the carpool at the end of the day, there's a big issue if the separation occurs early in the day. The employee may be stuck. Likewise, if the separation notification happens minutes before the on-site child-care center closes, the separated employee may be rushed to pick up a child. The most decent approach is to assign someone—a person from HR or an outplacement consultant—to help resolve logistical issues for that day. This person should check in with the employee as soon as he or she has gained composure to eliminate as much logistical stress as possible.

We encourage our readers to overestimate the amount of choreography that has to go into a well-planned, sensitive, and decent separation notification. Decency begins with training the managers. It involves selecting the right time and place for the notifications and having the right support systems in place immediately after the notifications. Decency also calls for support of the notification managers throughout their difficult day. While some companies have the staff and skills to attend to all these details themselves, an increasing number of companies turn to career management companies to handle the planning and immediate ramifications of notifications. Company managers have to notify the employees personally. But career management companies can be choreographers to help them put the pieces together with effectiveness and civility.

The Failure to Coordinate

One way to emphasize the need for planning is to show what can happen when important decency details are not considered in advance. The following is illustrative: Walmart, the largest company in the United States, also owns Sam's Club. On the same day in 2018 that Walmart proudly announced it was raising the minimum wage of its workers, awarding bonuses, and increasing maternity and paternity leave benefits, Sam's Club closed 53 stores with no announcement. Sam's Club employees showed up to open stores only to find that the doors were barred shut.

Analysts speculated that Sam's Club executives hoped they could avoid the bad news by "burying" the store closings on a day when the media would be focused on the good news from parent company Walmart. If so, they were sadly mistaken. Analysts were scathing in their reaction. "Sam's Club is trying to pull the wool over people's eyes," said Ed Zitron, founder of the media relations company EZPR. "They just made a rapid miscalculation."[2]

The lesson here is that in today's interconnected world, you should always assume that layoffs will go public about two minutes after the first person learns of it. The decision to keep employees in the dark resulted in hundreds of angry workers who turned to Facebook and Twitter to report their dilemma in real time. Traditional media love conflict, so they quickly picked up on the story. Many Sam's Club workers learned of this development from Facebook and Twitter before they heard it from their managers. What effect do you think this sequence had on employee engagement and loyalty?

Walmart leadership, by their own hand, missed the opportunity to have coordinated the events, to have statements ready to go, and to release them to the media simultaneously with the first notifications. And those notifications should have taken place personally.

The Decent Notification

The conversation between a manager and person being separated is the most critical element of the separation event. Two core management decencies are associated with this conversation:

- Take time with the employee. A short, rushed, or interrupted meeting is salt in the wound.
- Listen to the employee with empathy and with judicious response. If you're anxious or defensive, it may be even harder to remain silent while the employee talks. It's impossible to listen and talk at the same time.

If the employee is critical of the company, you should avoid debating the issue. Listening is different than agreeing.

You can forget a performance review when separating an employee; in fact, there could be consequences to relating a layoff to performance, however indirectly. Skip the reflective philosophical conversations and platitudes such as, "I know how you must feel," or "This is as difficult for me as it is for you." Rather, a brief conversation, to the point, delivered courteously and succinctly, will communicate the reality of the decision that is irrevocable. If confirmation of the employee's severance entitlements is delivered in writing at the same time, it avoids the potential for misunderstanding.

Separation Language

What words apply to individuals who are let go? The choice of words can reflect a company's attitude. An organization that talks about "terminees" or "rightsized employees" is likely to send a different message than one that uses words such as "former colleagues" or "separated employees." When someone at W. L. Gore & Associates quits or is let go, the company refers to it as a separation. "This word acknowledges that a mind and a heart are leaving the organization, and it speaks to the relationship side of the separation instead of only to the procedure," write Scott Cawood and Rita Bailey in *Destination Profit*. The separation of an employee can best be experienced as part of an organization's reputation bank account. Sometimes there are deposits, and sometimes there are withdrawals. Each separation should be treated directly, with candor, honesty, and sensitivity.

In any case, the objective should be less about finding the perfect euphemism and more about avoiding expressions that stray from the truth. Euphemisms are likely to backfire. Here are a few most of us are familiar with:

- Downsized
- Made redundant
- Streamlined
- Rightsized
- Asked to resign
- Coerced transition
- Decruited
- Dehired
- Force reduction
- Involuntary separation
- Released

What all these terms have in common is an attempt to avoid the reality that a business unilaterally terminated a worker's employment.

The reference statement should be carefully thought through. This is the language that the ex-employer will release to parties considering hiring the separated employee. It is almost always in everyone's interest to negotiate the content of this statement. Barring criminal activity, egregious behavior, or actions that will clearly involve further legal activity or bad publicity, the former company's position is that it would like to see the separated employee reemployed as quickly as possible. The former employee, of course, would usually like to be reemployed as quickly as possible. The reference statement should not be an obstacle to this shared interest. The content of the separation statement should be negotiated as generously as the facts permit. Human resources and former managers should be trained to release the separation statement without further comment or embellishment.

Tell the Truth

Telling the truth requires two separate commitments. First is the commitment to accept the truth for oneself. Second is the commitment to tell the truth to others. The first commitment is often the hardest.

Whether speaking with those being separated or those being retained, managers must be truthful, even when either party would prefer to say something else. While it might be tempting to tell a separated employee that there may be another job for him or her in a few months, that's rarely the truth and will only heighten expectations and discourage people from finding new work quickly. Retained employees want a commitment that they will not be next, but it is dangerous to make such promises. No matter how much it seems to hurt in the short term, in the long run it is always less painful to have heard the truth up front.

Using facts is a helpful way to deliver the truth. This may not always be convenient. Sometimes the facts are unpalatable. Nevertheless, both separated and retained employees are better off in an authentic relationship where all parties embrace the facts. Everyone, whether separated or still employed, needs to take individual responsibility for his or her job security and career destiny. It's impossible to do so without candid, fact-based conversations.

To summarize, the minimum requirements for decency in employee separation include the following five values:

1. A fair and preferably transparent selection process. This means objective, easily understood standards available for everyone to read.
2. Sensitive, in-person coaching of the terminating manager.
3. Sensitivity to the logistics of the notification process.
4. Clarity around exactly what the company will tell potential employers. This reference statement should be in writing so both parties are in sync.
5. Management accessibility to surviving employees.

Redeployment

Very simply, redeployment in the business context can be defined as the transfer of an employee to another position within the same organization.

This internal job transfer process is sometimes considered when there is a planned reduction in force and where the employer views redeployment as culture enhancing and affordable. Ours is a book on decency, civility, and respect in a business context. Our insights and observations on institutional redeployment relate to the process as a potentially value-added, culture-enrichment, and reputation-enhancing activity.

Among the success factors of redeployment are these:

- A moral commitment by leadership to invest in retaining as many employees as possible during a business downturn
- A policy and process steering committee composed of HR, IT, Finance, and Operations
- A commitment to "walking before running"—a pilot program accompanied by clear expectation setting and forthright communication
- An earnest commitment to job-transfer, onboarding, and, where necessary, retraining
- An up-to-date talent and skills inventory
- A commitment to eliminate or minimize talent hoarding by managers

- A directive requiring that internally displaced employees be prioritized over external candidates for rehiring

Leadership's commitment to a workforce redeployment strategy conveys two important messages: talent is a precious, limited resource, and it's less than moral or prudent to turn a blind eye to talent disposability. Inevitably, a redeployment policy will highlight a familiar ambivalence among line managers who want to move quickly in response to sudden changes in business conditions. Most companies in the United States have yet to consider redeployment in a scalable, holistic manner.

Separation Makes Memories

Saying goodbye is sometimes a business reality. The decencies associated with the details of how we say goodbye become an important component of a corporate culture. When we separate people, we are making memories: memories for those separated and memories for the cultures that will survive them. A clear testimony to a culture of trust is how a company separates valued people. "We hate to see you go. Give us your cell phone and keys to the company car. Security will escort you out!" These sentences sometimes need to be said. Of course, companies need to protect their assets. But it is neither decent nor prudent to use sloppy language during a separation episode.

The company should certainly protect itself by canceling passwords and retrieving keys, ID cards, cell phones, pagers, and so forth. But these steps need to be choreographed thoughtfully and in proportion to the situation. When an employee is fired for cause, such as embezzlement or harassment, it is entirely prudent for the company to block his or her access to networks and escort the employee off the premises. Any employee who has broken faith with the company cannot expect anything less. But if it's a no-fault separation where there is no issue surrounding the employee's performance or integrity, then decency calls for a different set of actions. In these cases, anything that questions the employee's performance or integrity can and should be avoided.

In all cases, security personnel should remain in the background unless the employee has demonstrated a lack of integrity or a propensity for acting out. If you have regard for the employee you are about to separate, ask yourself this question: "Would I rehire this person if I could?" If the answer is yes, then the risk is worth taking. Let such people gather their personal possessions in dignity and in private. Is there a risk here? Sure. Behaving well is no guarantee that someone else will not behave badly. But it's the way to go.

CHAPTER 9

THE INCIDENT AT HARKINS INDUSTRIES

Case Study: Leadership Recovery with Decency and Integrity Following a Damaging Incident

By James E. Lukaszewski, America's Crisis Guru®

Harkins Industries*

Corporate Profile
- Private Company
- Headquarters: Chicago
- Branches: Across the United States
- 35,000 employees
- Average Employee Education Level: High School, High School Diploma
- Management: B.A./B.S. Minimum Requirement. Advanced degrees are increasing in number
- Known For: Honesty, Integrity, Responsiveness, Hiring Veterans and Rehabilitated Prisoners
- CEO: Tim Harkins
- Founded: 1996
- Status: Likely to be acquired by a British conglomerate
- Motto: Helping America Succeed at Every Level

*Fictitious Company Name

For Tom Harkins, longtime CEO of Chicago-based multinational Harkins Industries, yesterday was the worst, most embarrassing day of his life. Two of his Texas recycling facilities were raided by the FBI representing the federal Environmental Protection Agency along with Texas State Police. Computers and documents were seized, and the plant manager at each facility received a subpoena.

As the raids were happening, Harkins was contacted by the Texas bureau of the *Wall Street Journal* and several Texas media outlets who, tipped off by police officials, were covering the raids as they occurred. The company specializes in recycling volatile liquid products. Harkins was recently featured in the *Wall Street Journal* for receiving a national award for hiring wounded veterans.

To reduce tedious reporting complexity, the local Harkins branch and several of its larger Texas regional customers, including a US Army base, had conspired to allow Harkins to round up quantities of liquids collected in certain cases, and round down in other cases, to standard volumes—quarts and gallons. They stopped reporting fractions of these quantities. These decisions were made below the contracting level at customer locations by local managers. However, the reports to the government are required to be exactly accurate, and false reporting is a crime. The CEO was alarmed that this story was going to blame the entire company when it was the act of a few local managers.

Senior management described the situation as a "sensationalized press issue." The company itself had never been the subject of any major adverse publicity. This became a national story, front-page news in several publications. The CEO's outrage convinced his internal staff that they needed to get help to resolve this "press problem."

I received a call from the company's Chicago head-quarters office alerting me that the CEO would be calling me directly. I was briefed on the situation. The caller told me that while the company's PR team was more than ade-quately experienced to handle the situation, the CEO insisted on using outside counsel. The caller's message was this:

1. The CEO didn't understand public relations and needed to learn the value of the function.
2. The CEO's current temperament was paralyzing senior management. He needed to be calmed down so that he could listen to reason.

Shortly after that call, the CEO was on the phone with me. "It was a press problem," he said. The press doesn't understand business, the CEO complained. This was a local issue caused by local managers. The company has always been known for its quality, integrity, and fair play. He pro-tested that the media exaggerated the facts and refused to hear the truth. At this point, it was clear that we were not going to get to the "what can you do for us" question anytime soon. I interrupted his self-righteous diatribe and simply asked him, "Mr. Harkins, whose name is on the door?"

Silence.

"It's *your* reputation that is at stake. It's going to be up to you and the company to put together an immediate strategy to deal honestly with the allegations being made by the *Wall Street Journal*."

Silence.

Then he said, "I'll think about it." And hung up.

My experience with these kinds of calls is that they're rarely returned, at least not immediately. I assumed that's what would happen here. The next morning, to my surprise, the CEO's assistant reached out to me and said the CEO would be calling me by the afternoon, with a much more reasonable tone.

A calmer and more rational CEO called by noon. "I've been thinking about what you told me, and I think you are right," he said. "Most of my leadership team has been adamant that you are wrong and that we need to come out swinging, or we'll look like sissies if we don't. I'm planning a road trip to all the branches to talk about the episode. I'm torn between what my colleagues want me to do and what you appear to be advising, so what's the plan? Our people believe the *Wall Street Journal* should apologize and retract parts of the story that we believe are flat-out wrong."

Here's essentially what I told him:

1. Forget the *Wall Street Journal*. The allegations are about you and your customers and your reputation.
2. You need to take concrete steps at the earliest possible time to reach out to all your stakeholders with a letter that accurately describes what happened and apologizes

for the breach of your own ethical standards and policies. You need to explain what you're learning from this situation, what you intend to do about it, and that you intend to keep them informed directly until the matter is resolved. I told him I would draft a proposed letter, send it to him, and that he should release it as quickly as possible. And, of course, copy the *Wall Street Journal* as well as other news outlets that have covered the company over the years, including trade journals.

The silence on the other end of the line was deafening, and his comment was, "This is going to be a tough sell to my colleagues." My response was, "Is *their* name on the door?"

The edited letter he sent back was a page longer than my draft. Harkins admitted that the story was entirely true. He added that he was ready to talk about the letter in person to anyone. His communications advisor called me, asked me if I was out of my mind, and said that this could spell the end of the company, that publicly shaming himself for something he had no direct responsibility for was something that would create a backlash! The entire management team was adamantly opposed to sending the letter.

The CEO, in one courageous act of leadership, sent the letter nevertheless. He called me to say he was awaiting the damning—perhaps ruinous—comments from all corners. I asked him to sit tight and to call with any reactions he was getting. The first reaction came via an e-mail from the *Wall Street Journal* reporter doing the story simply saying, "pretty gutsy . . . that's more like it!" The CEO was dumbfounded.

By the end of the week he'd called or heard directly from each of his major customers in the Texas region. All were congratulatory compliments, and no one mentioned the *Wall Street Journal*. They applauded the company's courage, transparency, and decency.

The CEO went on the road, visited each company operation, and universally achieved hero status. He thought about how this situation, which had at first seemed devastating, could be used to prevent this circumstance from ever occurring again. Over the next few months the company executives initiated a Code of Conduct process and reviewed and enhanced their company values statement.

Broader Lessons this Story Illustrates

1. Ethical leadership, responsiveness, courage, truthfulness, and decency are required and expected most during emergency situations and crises.

2. A crisis is an event that is people-stopping, show-stopping, product-stopping, and reputationally redefining that creates victims and often explosive visibility. The operative word in this definition and the most important by-product are the "victims."

3. In our experience all questionable, inappropriate, insidious, unethical, immoral, predatory, improper, victim-producing, and criminal behaviors are intentional. It's also true that all ethical, moral, compassionate, decent, civil, and lawful behaviors are also intentional. Those who lead always have a choice.

Six Leadership Recovery Strategies that Establish Trust After a Crisis

There is a definite pattern of recovery behaviors that helps leadership reestablish trust following a trust-busting, reputation-redefining circumstance. The message is this: when a trust-busting situation occurs, get trust recovery strategies working immediately, so the uncertainty, doubt, and fear that loss of trust creates can be eliminated more quickly.

1. **Stop producing victims and critics.** Change your behavior, your language, your vocabulary; recognize the power victims have to further damage your reputation and trusted relationships.
2. **Build/rebuild followership.** Reconnect, reestablish, and reconvene with those who are critical to building and recovering your leadership and trust.
3. **Build trust at every opportunity.** Trust must be vocalized; trust must be explained, expected, and modeled.
4. **Rebuild and maintain your base.** Focus initially on those closest to you—employees, retirees, their families—as well as those with whom the organization has relationships.
5. **Manage the victim dimension.** Victims and critics will outlive you. They are always with you. Pay attention to them, literally, until they no longer care. Failure to do this often reignites their victimization, their criticisms, and your untrustworthiness.

6. **Manage your own destiny.** Everything said, written, broadcast, or otherwise created about you and your organization now lives forever. You need a strategy to correct, clarify, and comment on the ethical observations of others. Failure to manage your own destiny leaves it to somebody else you may not even know. There always seems to be somebody ready to do it for you if you fail or delay doing it for yourself.

Remember your post-crisis recovery mantra: Decency requires a commitment to verbal and written communication that is predominantly positive and declarative. The associated behaviors should be simple, sensitive, sensible, constructive, positive, helpful, and empathetic. Any other pathways lead to trouble, prolong problems, and delay mitigation and resolution. In this context, empathy means positive deeds that speak louder and more constructively than words. The conventional wisdom about empathy, demonstrating that you understand the emotions and feelings of the victims, comes off as disingenuous and self-forgiving.

Five Elements to Leading with Civility, Decency, and Trust

Over the years, five crucial leadership strategies have emerged that deliver the personal power to move people and organizations into the future, while also being the model and setting the standard for trustable leadership with decency and honor.

Leadership with decency is the force that drives, nurtures, energizes, inspires, and attracts individuals, organizations, cultures, even societies to move forward every day. Adopt these five leadership strategies into your work and life every day, and you will be much more influential, important, happy, and successful. Those around you will noticeably improve their own personal and professional situations as a result of your example. Actively teaching others what you are doing will help them answer for themselves questions you know they will encounter along the way

These five strategies, applied with sincerity, are simple, sensible, constructive, positive, and doable. Taken together, they foster positive, decency-driven behaviors. This is the real work of leaders, providing the "how," the "what," and the "why" of getting things done. Using these strategies will also provide the framework for work-life satisfaction predicated on a foundation of decency.

1. Be Positive

An attitude of positivity is the single most profound and powerful change you can make in your life that will cause continuous positive change in the lives of others:

- Use positive, declarative language.
- Eradicate negative words and phrases.
- Reduce the use of emotional language.

It's tempting to dismiss these practices as simplistic. We've learned that taking this positive approach to work and life has a profound impact, because decency and integrity are profoundly positive concepts and aspirations. This strategy works in every culture we have experienced. How often have you approached your manager with an idea only to hear, "That's not the way we do things around here," or "We tried that five years ago and it failed; it won't work now either"? How did you feel? How likely were you to volunteer ideas in the future? Negative comments almost always put us on the defensive even though we have important, positive, and constructive things to say and propose.

2. Be Constructive

- Eliminate criticism as a method of correction, clarification, or coaching. Criticisms are negative, and they can cause permanent damage and victimization. All criticism is remembered negatively and emotionally forever. "Constructive" criticism is a toxic oxymoron.
- Insist on constructive behavior, language, and ideas even during arguments.
- Seek to make and solicit positive, constructive suggestions.
- Accept only constructive performance analysis of others.

Here's a story about criticism. A director of an organization sent the staff an e-mail requesting "constructive criticism" of the CEO. In due course, the director received hundreds of responses. The cumulative effect was devastating. The director was in a quandary. If the criticisms were presented, there was no way the CEO could possibly continue in the job. Nor could the director simply sit on the feedback. The director approached us for our advice.

The strategy we recommended was for the director to go back to the staff and, rather than asking for criticism, ask them to make one positive constructive suggestion about what the CEO might do to help them achieve the goals of the organization. The director eventually received fewer than a dozen well-considered and actionable responses. The CEO was grateful for the effort, took the feedback to heart, and worked to implement every recommendation.

The lesson here is an important one. The goal is, rather than providing lots of suggestions, provide only important, positive, and constructive ones. Providing criticism only harms and confuses those who need help. When you criticize, it authorizes others to criticize as well. You can unleash a torrent of ill feeling for which you get the blame. This strategy works at any level of an organization.

3. Focus on Outcomes

Stephen Covey was right: Begin with the end in mind. Commit to generating and maintaining forward momentum.

- Focus on today and tomorrow.
- Think and work in the future tense.

- Recognize that the past generally is more often debatable than helpful.
- Select achievable, understandable, time-sensitive, worthwhile goals; then go for them.

4. Communicate Intentionally

The main lesson we've learned about communication over the years is that it's more important to have a simple, general set of standards and attributes than to customize communications to specific audiences for specific purposes. We call this communicating intentionally. We call these "intentions" because this is how we seek to operate in daily life and to teach others to do the same. These are behaviors and beliefs that build trust. At the same time, this approach defines our ethical approach to life and to work, and our response to trouble. These are the main ingredients of decency, especially after a crisis:

Candor. Truth with an attitude, delivered now (the building block of trust):

- Disclose important information early.
- Explain your reasoning and reasons continuously.
- Discuss options and alternatives that you have considered.
- Provide unsolicited helpful information.

Openness, accessibility. Be available for the disasters as well as the ribbon cuttings, and be willing to respond.

Truthfulness in crisis. Lukaszewski's definition: Truth is 15 percent facts and data, 85 percent emotion and point of reference:

- Point of reference matters more than facts; determine which facts matter.
- In crisis, all facts will be debatable.
- Factual overload victimizes people and makes them feel stupid, and they may find their own experts to debate the facts presented.
- Too many facts destroy the ability to be humble.
- Special note: Harkins's letter to customers and others worked because it focused on admission, contrition, and apology, but still laid out facts that mattered.

During a crisis most management focus tends to be on defending and explaining by using facts. When the facts overwhelm acts of decency, integrity, and compassion, victims are traumatized, and additional critics are created.

Unconditional honesty, from the start.

Empathy. Actions that speak louder than words.

Responsiveness. Answering questions candidly in every situation, including setbacks, validates your integrity:

- Every concern or question, regardless of the source, is legitimate and must be addressed.

- Answer every question; avoid judging the questioner.
- Avoid taking any question personally.

Transparency. Avoid secrets, because important facts will always come out.

Engagement. Face-to-face is the communications approach desired by just about everyone including every victim.

Destiny management. It's your destiny, which only you can manage in your own best interest. Relentlessly correct, clarify, and comment rather than waiting for someone else to do it for you. The wrong people often show up and get you in deeper trouble.

Apology. The atomic energy of decency, apologies tend to stop bad things from starting, including litigation. Leaving any element out or adding in self-forgiveness or excuses invalidates the inherent positive power of apology:

- Acknowledge personal responsibility for having injured, insulted, failed, or wronged another.
- Explain what happened and the known reasons for the circumstance.
- Talk about what you and your organization have learned that will help prevent it from ever happening again.
- Sincerely ask for forgiveness in exchange for more appropriate future behavior and making amends.
- Make restitution.

5. Relentlessly Seek Positive, Incremental Personal Improvement Every Day

Invite everyone around you to follow your example. Most everything we do, know, or create came into being incrementally, occasionally leading to important breakthroughs, which are often too few and far between.

Leaders who practice incremental improvement daily automatically ask themselves several questions at the end of each day or throughout each day. This is a discipline that will ensure that even your most frustrating day produces some useful results:

1. What's the most important thing I learned today?
2. What's the most interesting thing I learned today?
3. What do I know now that I didn't know when I came to work this morning?
4. How many people did I help today, from their perspective?
5. What questions arose today that require answers or responses? When?
6. What will I change tomorrow based on what I learned today?

Trust Matters

> *"Trust is the absence of fear, and*
> *fear is the absence of trust."*
> **—JAMES E. LUKASZEWSKI**

Great Place to Work coproduces the annual *Fortune* magazine "100 Best Places to Work" rankings (see Chapter 7).

Trust is the most important criterion in identifying the winning corporate cultures, and those companies rise to the top in terms of financial performance. Professor Nicholas Epley, in his article "How to Design an Ethical Organization," proposed that employees are likely to behave differently if they think the organization is being guided by the ethics of Mr. Rogers, the relentlessly kind PBS show host, versus that of Gordon Gekko, the relentlessly greedy financier in the film *Wall Street*.[1]

Avoid These Trust-Busters, the Enemies of Decency

Entire books have been written on trust. For our purposes, trust means confidence that the other party will act in an expected manner. Trust is the absence of fear, and fear is the absence of trust. It's often easier to talk about trust-busters, behaviors that destroy trust. Here is a partial but useful list of trust-busters:

- **Arrogance.** The absence of empathy. Taking action without consulting those directly or indirectly affected. Making decisions unilaterally, without important input from key stakeholders.
- **Broken promises.** One of the crucial bases of trust is that each party can rely on the commitments of the other, both implicit and explicit. When those commitments are broken without prior notification, understanding, explanation, and warning, the first element of the relationship to suffer is trust. Losing

the sense of commitment can call into question most other elements of the relationship as well.

- **Chest-beating—mindless, needless, and useless bragging.** Unwarranted self-congratulatory, self-validating behavior puts distance between those who want to be trusted and those who need to trust. It is a form of self-deception through self-talk. It is reasonable for a company to be proud of its achievements but take care that the emphasis is more on the achievements than the pride.
- **Deception—intentionally misleading through omission, commission, negligence, or incompetence.** In a relationship, deception creates a feeling of separation and distance. Deception also creates a sense of disappointment because the individual, product, company, or organization failed to recognize that, at the very least, there should be a sense of candor between the parties no matter what the circumstance.
- **Denial.** When a product underperforms or there is an injury, the temptation is to conclude that the problem may not be as serious as it appears. Denial is always a costly mistake. Failing to promptly come forward and relate the circumstances candidly, with empathy for those who are affected, changes a relationship of trust into one of suspicion and caution.
- **Disparagement.** Anytime you hear such phrases as "They have their own agenda," or "He's uninformed," or "They're just looking to raise money by their

action," or "It's politically motivated," or "They just don't understand," you immediately suspect that the exact opposite is true, and you're likely to be right. All critics and opponents have friends elsewhere. Some of those friends are your friends as well. Victory is never achieved through disparagement. Disparagement causes suspicion, damages relationships, and creates permanent critics. Enemies accumulate.

- **Disrespect.** Even adversaries can trust each other, to some extent, if there is respect. When an individual, product, or organization is minimized, trivialized, or humiliated, there is a sense of uneasiness and discomfort that leads to frustration, anger, and public negative response.
- **Failure to seek forgiveness or to apologize.** Often even the best public and private approaches are diminished in value when, either for reasons of arrogance or stubbornness, an organization avoids a direct, overt approach for seeking forgiveness from the parties harmed or indirectly affected. Failure to quickly say, "We're sorry" diminishes trust and leads to litigation.
- **Holding back.** Deliberately withholding support, withholding admiration, withholding cooperation and collaboration, but especially withholding information corrodes trust.
- **Lying.** Often starting with simple misunderstandings, the truth to one individual or organization can easily seem untruthful to a victim, competitor, critic,

or angry neighbor. Truth can be complicated and emotional.

- **Self-forgiveness.** This is self-talk designed to ignore reality. Symptoms of self-forgiveness include such self-serving phrases as "Mistakes can happen, even to the best companies," "We've been paying taxes in this community for decades," "I didn't know what was going on," "No one told me," "We're only human," or "People make mistakes." Self-forgiveness destroys trust.

- **Victim confusion.** Avoid exhibiting an irritable reaction to reporters, employees, angry neighbors, and victims' families when they call asking for help, information, an explanation, or an apology, such as "We've been a good corporate citizen," or "We've contributed to the opera, the little league, the shelter program," or "We don't deserve to be treated badly." All of these answers say, "Hey! We're victims, too." These behaviors are an attack on the credibility and honesty of real victims. It's accusatory and destructive.

The Decency Code: A Leader's Pathway to Integrity and Trust

Ethical expectations of leaders are present in cultural settings, families, businesses and work, communities, and whole societies. What's remarkable is the simplicity, similarity, and power of these expectations, wherever we see them, including during crises. The information in this chapter applies everywhere. Ethical expectations of leadership are present and required, whether these expectations are recognized at first or not. Most leaders will ultimately be held accountable for their ethical performance. Fortunately for us during our careers, in several important cases employee groups were polled and systematically interviewed about their ethical expectations of leadership during adverse times. The nine ethical expectations they mentioned as necessary to maintaining ethical and decent cultures we find frequently duplicated around the world:

1. Find the truth as soon as possible: Tell that truth and act on it.
2. Promptly raise the tough questions and answer them thoughtfully. This includes asking and answering questions yet to be asked or thought of by those who will be affected by whatever the circumstance is.
3. Teach by parable. Illustrate or underscore self-evident truths, principles, or moral lessons.
4. Clarify; then vocalize core business values and ideals constantly.
5. Walk the talk. Be accessible; help people understand the organization within the context of its values and ideals at every opportunity.
6. Help, expect, and enforce ethical leadership.
7. Preserve, protect, defend, and foster access to the top of the organization.

8. Be a cheerleader, model, teacher, and coach of ethical behavior.
9. Make values more important than (or at least equal to) profits.

Our interpretation of these ethical expectations is the essence of *The Decency Code* and form a leader's pathway to integrity and trust.

A CLOSING PERSPECTIVE FROM THE AUTHORS

Congratulations. However you got here, whether you read the book, skimmed the book, or just came directly to this page, we hope the topic has been of interest and helpful to you as you explore this ever-more-important subject.

Despite jail terms and fines, a tougher legal environment, thousands of books on leadership, university courses on ethics, multiple "great place to work" lists, and theories on what it takes to create vibrant corporate cultures, significant progress on the goal of building decent workplaces—places in which employees feel proud to bring their whole selves—is difficult to see. Misconduct continues; workplace incivility continues. And if we are making progress on employee engagement, it can be best described as baby steps. Our book, we hope, offers some practical steps to the goal of decent workplaces we all desire.

Throughout this book, we emphasized concepts of civility, respect, and decency, rather than regulation alone, as the antidote to disrespect and disengagement. Decency is more than just "tone at the top" (as critical as leadership from the top is), but tone at all levels at all times in all contexts, especially when it is thought that no one is watching. These attributes in turn are the main ingredients of an ethical, compliant, and productive culture.

We selected the term "decency" for this book because we wanted a word that reflects our view that small, constructive institutionalized gestures build great companies, families, and communities. It follows that developing and enabling a civil environment helps fortify a company against misconduct. By fertilizing the foundation of corporate cultures with decencies, there's a likelihood that real engagement will improve, and a better than even chance that compliance initiatives can more easily take root.

Decencies serve a culture by adding impact to ethical standards. Leaders play a prominent role in this process. When the "little things"—small yet meaningful gestures—take hold, they create stories and traditions that can enrich a culture. They can be felt by everyone. They are a unifying set of experiences that coalesce into resilient, value-driven cultures, resistant to the corner-cutting that is preliminary to serious misconduct. It turns out that "little things" have a much bigger impact than we generally imagine and often last a long time.

We also observe that groups of small decencies tend to have a synergistic impact. That is, when you add the small decencies together, their impact is much larger than expected.

A leader's commitment to a civil and enabling business environment is essential. Small decencies—gestures that are visible, actionable, and scalable—are part of that commitment. Woven into the fabric of a corporate culture, the following acts make the concepts of respect and integrity more vivid and palpable: leadership accessibility and transparency; nonfinancial rewards ("psychic income") such as exhibiting trust and handwritten notes of thanks or job-well-done; downsizing with empathy, sympathy, sensitivity, candor, honesty, and continuously constructive communication when downsizing is necessary; banning executive pomposity and pretentious perks and demonstrating the power of humility.

Every absence of decency where decency is needed dilutes the culture of an organization. The stories that a company tells about itself are critical. Institutionalized decency gives everyone in the organization important clues about what its values are and how committed it is to the expression of these values.

We believe there is cause for optimism. After all, an ethics industry has been born, complete with a global association, the Society of Corporate Compliance and Ethics (SCCE). Important new roles have been created: chief compliance officer, chief ethics officer, chief corporate social responsibility officer. There are fewer "celebrity CEOs." Some corporate "bad guys" are paying their dues in jail. Character, integrity, and humility are still valued leadership attributes. Business ethics is beginning to work its way into major business school curricula and MBA programs. Reputation impact is a growing corporate priority. Beyond *Fortune* magazine's 100 Best Places to Work, there's *Fortune*'s World's Most Admired Companies, *Ethisphere* magazine's World's Most Ethical Companies, *Trust Across America*'s America's Top 10 Most Trustworthy Public Companies, and *CRO Magazine*'s American's 100 Best Corporate Citizens.

Decency and Civility Powerfully Enrich a Culture

The role of decency and civility enriches and toughens a corporate culture. You could argue that it is exactly the goodwill built up by decencies that allows an organization to make it through the tough times.

Culture enrichment gives an organization sustainability and an employer-of-choice reputation, and, yes, it even promotes regulatory compliance. Cultural enrichment is about getting a uniformly positive response to the question, "How does it feel to live in this environment and be shaped by it?"

The new world of work is about speed, agility, work-life balance, virtuality, globalization, multigenerational workforces, artificial intelligence, nontraditional work styles, CSR/sustainability, and safety and security. Each of these workplace components requires culture-focused ethical and engaging leadership. Global competition for increasingly scarce talent has challenged the best of companies. Workplaces that have enabling cultures where innovation is stimulated, where performance is recognized, and where employee engagement thrives will be the winners.

Leadership with the Right Stuff Will Be the Key

The well-studied leadership attributes—vision, courage, trust, optimism, inspiration, humility, communication—are important. But more is required to succeed as a leader of the future. Leaders must also be authentic, adaptable, globally savvy, environmentally savvy, socially savvy (EQ), compliance-savvy, and future-focused. A decencies tool kit will be needed that can detect, prevent, remove, or deter avoidable management trip wires. These are those management fumbles, stumbles, and bungles that make people scratch their heads and triggers the question, "What were you thinking?"

Used effectively, this tool kit and the other attributes we've mentioned can help inoculate a culture and its management against misconduct and incivility.

We are especially captivated by leaders who inspire, create visions, and then transform vision into action:

- **The late Herb Kelleher, founder and CEO of Southwest Airlines.** "The important thing is to take the bricklayer and make him understand that he's building a home, not just laying bricks."
- **The late Warren Bennis.** "Leadership may be the greatest performing art of all—the only one that

creates institutions of lasting value . . . institutions that can endure long after the stars who envisioned them have left the theater."

- **Daniel Goleman.** "Great leaders move us. They ignite our passion and inspire the best in us. When we try to explain why they are so effective, we speak of strategy, vision or powerful ideas; but the reality is much more primal. Great leadership works through emotions."
- **Charles Schwab.** "I want our employees to see themselves not as workers at a discount brokerage firm but rather as custodians of their customers' financial dreams."

Strength in Humility

Great leaders see the strength in humility, sharing the limelight and catching people doing things right. They have a passion for stamping out demotivators that can suck life and energy out of an organization. They make room for innovators and give them permission to fail.

And during turbulent times, great leaders avoid at all cost evidence and symbols of hypocrisy or mixed messages. They exhibit an unflagging sense of purpose. They're accessible, on deck, listening to people, being visible or accessible everywhere, even off-hours. They are promise keepers. They tell people what they know and what they don't know, and they convey a sense of hope. It's these habits that foster and build employee engagement. These are leaders with integrity.

Understanding What Employee Engagement Means

Joe Murphy, one of the true gurus of the global compliance community, in a private conversation with the authors reminds us that the key to understanding how to make employee engagement work is understanding the logical differences between how management views employee engagement and how employees view employee engagement. Most employees look at their work through the prism of their home life—including getting home on time. They work to live. Management from middle to top increasingly tends to look at work through the prism of the work that needs to be done—frankly, how to get more done in the limited time that employees are available. In today's business world the more successful managers become, the more their life is determined by the work to be done, excluding most other factors in their lives, even family life.

The leader who creates engagement understands the home and family orientation of employees. That leader tells employees what they want to know, don't know, need to know, and should know before they have to know these things. Advance information like this builds trust. The engaging leader listens, is accessible, and helps employees better understand how to explain over the supper table how their work relates to their family and home life. Engaged employees feel part of an organization whose leaders understand and value the relationship between work, family, and home life.

Implicit Bias Is Better Understood

These days, implicit bias is at the root of much of what creates problems in the workplace. To control implicit bias, we're learning to name the behaviors of concern. Unconscious bias contributes to the unfair treatment of minority groups in the workplace because individuals with power are generally not aware of their biases. Explicit bias is often acknowledged and sometimes defended. Even the act of denying that explicit bias is operating in the moment acknowledges that the bias is real.

An ethical and civil culture is the sum of the tangible, homegrown, specific behaviors and time-honored traditions that form the fabric of an organization, help ensure its sustainability, and help reduce its vulnerability. It's one way of saying, "That's how we do things around here." Another term for these behaviors is "small decencies." When C-suite leaders tell us, "That works for me," we'll know we've arrived!

The Future Is Watching

As Doris Kearns Goodwin, in her article "How to Find a Good Leader," says (with "he" intended to mean both "he" and "she"), "A leader is aware he is the object of many eyes. This puts a responsibility on him to act in a certain way— with respect for his own dignity and yours. Even if he's not in the mood, he must uphold standards of presentation.

Children are watching and taking cues. That means the future is watching."[1]

Two of the most important leadership characteristics are integrity and a sense of purpose. In a turbulent world, effective leadership acts as a stabilizer. Decency, we have argued in this book, is the attribute that controls the thermostat for a corporate culture. Decency can only develop in an environment of trust. Jim Lukaszewski has a simple definition of trust: the absence of fear. Therefore, fear is the absence of trust. People who trust will follow, and every leader knows it is committed followers who will help them accomplish the goals they aspire to achieve.

People who love their jobs have a sense of purpose. They feel valued and are energized to contribute thoughtfully to the success of their teams and organization. Employees are looking for meaning. Part of the responsibility of managers and leaders alike is to see and hear each employee's unique purpose and values, help them develop a plan to achieve their goals, and foster relationships built on trust and honest feedback. When leaders see and acknowledge their employees as whole people, whose primary concerns are about home and family first, employee engagement becomes an enrichment of the human experience.

We started this segment suggesting that the progress corporate America has been making on the path to decency-driven employee engagement is best described as baby steps. Maybe so. But we can make the entire journey that way.

* * *

The Decency Code leads to a multitude of pathways, all of which end in decency, civility, and integrity. While it's true that decency in many respects is a personal matter, what is abundantly clear from our experience is that, in organizations of any kind, leadership drives the beliefs, behaviors, and expectations of everyone else. The organization that has made its way toward decency is the organization that facilitates and is happy to see employees have productive, inspiring, and useful private lives. The organization whose culture works to overcome the barriers to decency and aligns more and more with *The Decency Code* is a culture where people want to work.

Thank you for joining us on this journey. We're easy to find if you'd like to talk further or have us talk to others about what you've learned from spending this time with us.

Steve Harrison
New York, New York
Steve.Harrison@LHH.com

James E. Lukaszewski
America's Crisis Guru®
Minneapolis, Minnesota
jel@e911.com
www.E911.com

NOTES

Chapter 1

1. H. Jackson Brown Jr., *Life's Little Instruction Book* (Rutledge Hill Press, 1991).

Chapter 2

1. Gallup, "State of the American Workforce," 2017, https://cloc .umd.edu/library/research/State%20of%20the%20American %20Workplace%202017.pdf.
2. Gallup, "State of the American Workforce," 2017, https://cloc .umd.edu/library/research/State%20of%20the%20American %20Workplace%202017.pdf.
3. Catherine Clifford, "Unhappy Workers Cost the U.S. Up to $550 Billion a Year," *Entrepreneur* magazine, May 10, 2015, https://www.entrepreneur.com/article/246036.
4. Elizabeth Doty, "Want to Change Corporate Culture? Focus on Actions.," *Strategy & Business*, March 15, 2019, https://www.strategy-business.com/blog/Want-to-change -corporate-culture-Focus-on-actions?gko=30cf7.
5. Doty, "Want to Change Corporate Culture?"
6. David M. Noer, *Healing the Wounds: Overcoming the Trauma of Layoffs and Revitalizing Downsized Organizations* (Jossey Bass Business & Management Series, 1995).
7. Global Workplace Analytics, "Latest Telecommuting/Mobile Work/Remote Work Statistics," August 16, 2019, https:// globalworkplaceanalytics.com/telecommuting-statistics.

8. Niraj Chokshi, "Out of the Office: More People Are Working Remotely, Survey Finds," *New York Times*, February 15, 2017, https://www.nytimes.com/2017/02/15/us/remote-workers-work-from-home.html.

9. Les Landes, "Getting to the Heart of Employee Engagement, Public Relations Tactics," Public Relations Society of America, June 2014, https://apps.prsa.org/Intelligence/Tactics/Articles/view/10667/1094/Getting_to_the_Heart_of_Employee_Engagement#.XYokxChKibg.

10. Kevin Kruse, "What Is Employee Engagement?," *Forbes*, June 22, 2012, https://www.forbes.com/sites/kevinkruse/2012/06/22/employee-engagement-what-and-why/#26723fd67f37.

11. Talent Management, "What Is Employee Engagement?," IBM Corporation, April 4, 2019, https://www.ibm.com/talent-management/hr-topic-hub/employee-engagement.

12. Gallup, "Employee Engagement Hierarchy," http://web.jhu.edu/administration/finance/initiatives/Employee_Engagement_Hierarchy.pdf.

13. Julie Gebauer and Don Lowman, *Closing the Engagement Gap: How Great Companies Unlock Employee Potential for Superior Results* (Portfolio, 2008), Kindle.

14. Lauren Weber, "Why Companies Are Failing at Reskilling," Management & Careers, *Wall Street Journal*, April 19, 2019, https://www.wsj.com/articles/the-answer-to-your-companys-hiring-problem-might-be-right-under-your-nose-11555689542.

15. Ethics Resource Center, *The Importance of Ethical Culture*, Supplemental Research Brief, 2009 National Business Ethics Survey, https://assets.corporatecompliance.org/portals/1/PDF/resources/surveys/244_0_1.pdf.

Chapter 3

1. Julia Bourke, Stacey Garr, Ardie van Berkel, and Julie Wong, "Diversity and Inclusion: The Reality Gap: 2017 Global Human Capital Trends," Deloitte, https://www2.deloitte.com/us/en/insights/focus/human-capital-trends/2017/diversity-and-inclusion-at-the-workplace.html.

Chapter 4

1. Julianne Pepitone, "U.S. Job Satisfaction Hits 22-Year Low," CNN Money, January 5, 2010, https://money.cnn.com/2010/01/05/news/economy/job_satisfaction_report/.
2. Mercer Talent Trends Study 2018 Global Findings, https://www.mercer.com/content/dam/mercer/attachments/global/Career/gl-2018-talent-trends-2018-infographic-global-mercer.pdf.
3. Christine Porath, "The Price of Incivility: Lack of Respect Hurts Morale and the Bottom Line," *Harvard Business Review*, January/February 2013, https://hbr.org/2013/01/the-price-of-incivility.
4. Bill Conerly, "Companies Need to Know the Dollar Cost of Employee Turnover," *Forbes*, August 12, 2018, https://www.forbes.com/sites/billconerly/2018/08/12/companies-need-to-know-the-dollar-cost-of-employee-turnover/#2cd405c4d590.
5. Sharon Florentine, "9 Reasons Good Employees Leave—and How You Can Prevent It," *CIO* magazine, June 8, 2019, https://www.cio.com/article/2858746/9-reasons-good-employees-leave-and-how-you-can-prevent-it.html.
6. Mayuri Chaudhary, "Growing Disconnect Between Employees and Employers," *HR Technologist*, May 16, 2017, https://www.hrtechnologist.com/news/performance-management-hcm/growing-disconnect-between-employees-and-employers/.
7. Jon Picoult, "Be Nice to Job Seekers. (They're Shoppers, Too.)," *New York Times*, May 30, 2009, https://www.nytimes.com/2009/05/31/jobs/31pre.html.
8. Picoult, "Be Nice to Job Seekers."

Chapter 5

1. Jon Picoult, "Be Nice to Job Seekers. (They're Shoppers, Too.)," *New York Times*, May 30, 2009, https://www.nytimes.com/2009/05/31/jobs/31pre.html.
2. H. Jackson Brown Jr., *Life's Little Instruction Book* (Rutledge Hill Press, 1991).

Chapter 6

1. Leslie Gaines-Ross, "Offices Can Be Bastions of Civility in an Uncivil Time," *Harvard Business Review*, July 14, 2017, https://hbr.org/2017/07/offices-can-be-bastions-of-civility-in-an-uncivil-time.

2. Ethics and Compliance Initiative, "Interpersonal Misconduct in the Workplace: What It Is, How It Occurs and What You Should Do About It," 2018 Global Business Ethics Survey, https://www.ethics.org/knowledge-center/2018-gbes-2/.

3. Ethics and Compliance Institute, *2018 Global Workplace Survey: Ethics & Compliance Programs*, June 28, 2018, https://www.ethics.org/press-release/global-workplace-survey-ethics-compliance-programs-create-significant-roi-improved-culture/.

4. John Kador, "A Little Rudeness Has Big Impacts on Corporate Culture," *Corporate Board Member*, https://boardmember.com/little-rudeness-big-impacts-corporate-culture/.

5. Kador, "A Little Rudeness Has Big Impacts on Corporate Culture."

6. Gallup, "Employee Engagement Hierarchy," http://web.jhu.edu/administration/finance/initiatives/Employee_Engagement_Hierarchy.pdf.

7. https://www.slideshare.net/reed2001/culture-1798664/2-Netflix_CultureFreedom_Responsibility2.

Chapter 7

1. Gallup, "State of the Workplace Report," 2017, https://www.gallup.com/workplace/238085/state-american-workplace-report-2017.aspx.

2. Zoe Mackey, "10 Startling Employee Engagement Statistics," BK Connection, Berrett-Koehler Publishers, January 11, 2019, https://ideas.bkconnection.com/10-startling-employee-engagement-and-statistics.

3. Mackey, "10 Startling Employee Engagement Statistics."

4. Mackey, "10 Startling Employee Engagement Statistics."

5. Matt Palmquist, "Workplace Perks: Wasteful Indulgence or Powerful Profit Driver?," *Strategy+Business*, August 20, 2018,

https://www.strategy-business.com/blog/Workplace-Perks
-Wasteful-Indulgence-or-Powerful-Profit-Driver?gko=3cb91.

6. Larry Fauver, Michael B. McDonald, and Alvaro G.
Taboada, "Does It Pay to Treat Employees Well? International Evidence on the Value of Employee-Friendly Culture,"
Journal of Corporate Finance 50 (June 2018), https://www
.researchgate.net/publication/323379204_Does_it_pay
_to_treat_employees_well_International_evidence_on_the
_value_of_employee-friendly_culture.

7. Fauver, McDonald, and Taboada, "Does It Pay to Treat
Employees Well?"

8. For example, Mark Emmons, "Key Statistics About Millennials in the Workplace," Dynamic Signal, https://resources
.dynamicsignal.com/ebooks-guides/speaking-millennial
?_ga=2.102145601.1790628551.1569349081-1158730446
.1569349081.

9. Deloitte, "The 2016 Deloitte Millennial Survey: Winning
over the Next Generation of Leaders," https://www2.deloitte
.com/content/dam/Deloitte/global/Documents/About
-Deloitte/gx-millenial-survey-2016-exec-summary.pdf.

10. Achieve, "Why Do Millennials Choose to Engage in Cause
Movements?," The Millennial Impact Report, http://www
.themillennialimpact.com/.

11. Cornerstone OnDemand, "Research Reveals the Driving
Force Behind American Employees and Their Career Choices,"
March 23, 2016, https://investors.cornerstoneondemand
.com/investors/news-and-events/news/news-details/2016
/Research-Reveals-the-Driving-Force-behind-American
-Employees-and-Their-Career-Choices/default.aspx.

12. Sarah Landrum, "Millennials Aren't Afraid to Change Jobs,
and Here's Why," *Forbes*, November 10, 2017, https://www
.forbes.com/sites/sarahlandrum/2017/11/10/millennials
-arent-afraid-to-change-jobs-and-heres-why/#2cc76c9b19a5.

13. For example, Victor Lipman, "65% of Employees Want More
Feedback (So Why Don't They Get It?)," *Forbes*, August
6, 2016, https://www.forbes.com/sites/victorlipman/2016/08
/08/65-of-employees-want-more-feedback-so-why-dont-they
-get-it/#c9bfc34914ad.

Chapter 8

1. Daniel Roth, "How to Cut Pay, Lay Off 8,000 People, and Still Have Workers Who Love You. It's Easy: Just Follow the Agilent Way," *Fortune*, February 4, 2002, https://money .cnn.com/magazines/fortune/fortune_archive/2002/02/04 /317477/index.htm.
2. Danielle Wiener-Bronner and Laura Sanicola, "Sam's Club Store Closings Are a PR Mess on Walmart's Big Day," CNNMoney, January 11, 2018, https://money.cnn.com/2018 /01/11/news/companies/walmart-sams-club-pr-mess/index .html.

Chapter 9

1. Nicholas Epley and Amit Kumar, "How to Design an Ethical Organization," *Harvard Business Review*, May-June 2019.

A Closing Perspective from the Authors

1. Peggy Noonan, "How to Find a Good Leader: Look for Someone with 'an Ambition for Self That Becomes an Ambition for Something Larger,'" *Wall Street Journal*, November 1, 2018, https://www.wsj.com/articles/how-to-find-a-good -leader-1541111329.

ACKNOWLEDGMENTS

We know what you're thinking, "Here comes a typical long list of barely recognizable names of the authors' relatives, friends, and networks who have had varying degrees of involvement in their book," but not this time! For sure, our immediate families, close friends, our advisor John Kador, and our clients and colleagues all have had meaningful influence and have made important contributions to this book. Lee Hecht Harrison CEO, Ranjit de Sousa, and Peter Alcide before him have modeled the type of leadership behavior that is advocated within these pages. We are genuinely grateful for this.

Despite being a "business book," the themes are relevant as well in everyday life at all levels, and in every societal circumstance. Decency, civility, respect, and trustworthiness are valued attributes, especially now with the advent of social media and the endless variety of message accelerants. Added to this mix are your coauthors whose career experiences are about conflict resolution, employee engagement, culture enrichment, and alignment with those committed to safe, nourishing, and rewarding workplaces. We are fortunate to have observed the byproduct of enlightened, ethical, and trustworthy leadership on display within the hundreds of great places to work in America and beyond.

INDEX

ABOUT THE AUTHORS

Stephen Harrison

Steve Harrison is a leading expert on careers and business ethics, an international speaker, and author of *The Manager's Book of Decencies: How Small Gestures Build Great Companies*, published by McGraw-Hill in 2007.

Steve is Vice Chairman of Lee Hecht Harrison, one of the world's largest and most respected global career management services companies. Lee Hecht Harrison is an operating company of Adecco, a $30 billion company with 33,000 full-time employees in 5,100 offices in 60 countries.

Steve served as the Worldwide Chief Compliance and Human Resources Officer of Adecco, the world's largest HR solutions company. He is also a past member of Adecco's Group Executive Management Committee.

In addition to serving as LHH's president, Steve has also held a range of Adecco positions, including Chief HR Officer, CEO of Adecco Career Services, and Chief Compliance Officer. Harrison received a BA from Lycoming

College and an MBA in Industrial Relations from the University of Cincinnati.

As an internationally recognized authority on career issues, corporate governance, and the human side of ethical business practices, Harrison frequently speaks in front of corporate audiences worldwide.

Steve lives in New York City with his psychologist wife, Shirley. He is the father of two daughters and a son. His hobbies include fly-fishing some of America's pristine waters. Steve may be contacted at Steve.Harrison@LHH .com.

James E. Lukaszewski

Jim Lukaszewski (Loo-ka-SHEV-skee) is one of America's most visible corporate go-to experts for senior executives when there is trouble in the room or on the horizon. As America's Crisis Guru®, Lukaszewski is known for his ability to help executives look at problems from a variety of sensible, constructive, and principled perspectives.

Lukaszewski has spent more than 40 years understanding the pathologies of management and leadership misbehaviors that lead to cultures of suspicion and error. Known as America's Crisis Guru®, he has guided nearly 300 American and international companies through more than 400 reputation redefining crises, over 40 years. *Lukaszewski on Crisis Communication* (2013), his latest book, is considered by many to be the CEO's survival guide for reputation risk and crisis management problems.

Every student of public relations or crisis management, anywhere in the world, usually sees, reads, studies, or is taught from something Jim has written or broadcast. He is the author of 13 books and hundreds of articles and monographs. His most recent books include:

- *Why Should the Boss Listen to You? The Seven Disciplines of the Trusted Strategic Advisor*, Jossey-Bass, 2009
- *Lukaszewski on Crisis Communication: What Your CEO Needs to Know About Reputation Risk and Crisis Management*, Rothstein Publishing, 2013
- *The Manager's Guide to Handling the Media in Crisis* (e-book), Rothstein Publishing, 2017

Since 1974, Jim has spent his career counseling leaders of all types who face challenging situations that often involve contention, conflict, controversy, community action, or activist opposition. He is known for taking a business approach rather than traditional PR strategies by teaching clients to take highly focused, ethically appropriate action. He is a consummate storyteller. Lukaszewski has helped leaders in organizations large and small in literally every sector, public and private. He is often retained by senior management to directly intervene and manage the resolution of corporate problems and bad news while providing personal coaching and executive recovery advice for executives in trouble or facing career-defining problems and succession or departure issues.

Jim works for a broad range of organizations including Fortune 100 companies, foundations, manufacturers, retail organizations, government organizations, associations, and NGOs. Jim's client list is confidential.

Jim's biography has appeared in more than 30 editions of various *Who's Who* annual editions. He has been recognized for lifetime achievement in his profession by most of the major public relations organizations in the United States. Jim served for 22 years on the Public Relations Society of America's Board of Ethics and Professional Standards (BEPS) and is now its first Emeritus member. Jim is based in Bloomington, Minnesota. Jim may be contacted at jel@e911.com or www.E911com.

More Crucial Reading
for Your Business Library

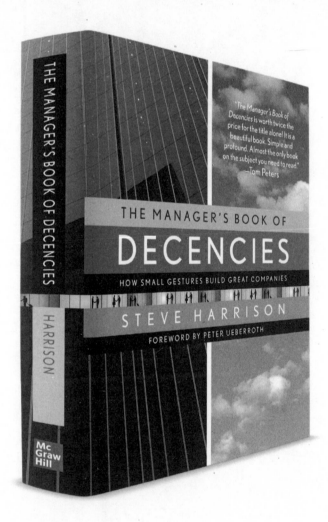